Railway Reflections

Railway Reflections

A Historical Review of Utah Railroads

Paintings by
Gilbert H. Bennett

Historical Narrative by
Stephen L. Carr

Ogden Union Station Foundation

www.theunionstation.org

Designed by
Gary Hidden

Graphics and typesetting by
Allan Davis and Betty Pletcher

Copyright © 1999 by
Ogden Union Station Foundation

Published by
Ogden Union Station Foundation
Ogden Union Station
2501 Wall Avenue
Ogden, Utah 84401

Library of Congress Cataloging-in-Publication Data
Carr, Stephen L.
  Railway reflections : an historical review of Utah railroads / paintings by Gilbert H. Bennett : historical narrative by Stephen L. Carr.
    p.cm.
  1. Railroads–Utah–History. 2. Railroads in art–Utah–History. I. Bennett, Gilbert H.
  1960- II. Title.

 HE2771.U7 .C37 1999
385'.0972–dc21
ISBN: 0-9674592-0-6

— Table of Contents —

— Foreword —

Punishing grades and brutal variations in climate plagued railroaders in Utah. The Rocky Mountains, criss-crossed with steep narrow canyons were an obstacle that would succumb only to the most ingenious engineers and persistent railroad builders. Extremes of both weather and terrain were, and continue to be, at odds with the railroads. Temperatures varied from 40 below zero atop grades that climbed to nearly 8,000 feet to the arid desert climates that afforded no water, yet plenty of heat and wind. Utah was not a region that would easily be shod by the iron rails.

Promontory Summit, Utah Territory, on May 10, 1869, is instilled in the memory of any student of American history. The *Jupiter* and the #119 nearly touched each other with the trainmen's arms outstretched in celebration with a symbolic toast. This was a fitting point for the culmination of this tremendous achievement, yet a place little different from any other location along this long, lonely road. It was significant because it foretold the pivotal role Utah even then began to play in the future of American railroading.

Railway Reflections tells the story of Utah railroads in a format that allows the reader to experience the triumph of man and machine through the eyes of one of America's premier railroad artists, Gil Bennett. Through Gil's art the reader relives the experiences, equipment, and locations that make Utah unique. His narrative shows what an artist thinks when he puts down on canvas his vision of events of a bygone era.

Dr. Stephen Carr, a noted Utah railroad historian gives us the facts behind the pictures and the story that bring the historic perspective to the reader. Steve, with his extensive knowledge of Utah railroads, defines the role that Utah and the railroads played regionally and nationally, demonstrating Utah's dynamic participation in America's westward expansion.

In a work such as this, numerous words, phrases and other technical information will occur which may be unfamiliar to many readers. Please refer to the glossary on pages 94 and 95 for simplified definitions.

I sincerely hope that you enjoy your trip into Utah's past with this book. Ogden, the home of the Utah State Railroad Museum, has long been known as Junction City, and as such has a deep railroad history. This book marks the first effort by the Utah State Railroad Museum at the Ogden Union Station to be involved in this kind of endeavor. The equipment depicted in many of the scenes is a part of the Museum collection. We welcome readers to stop and enjoy the museum and its collection.

Robert Geier
Executive Director,
Ogden Union Station

— Preface —

Utah—the name comes from the Ute Indian word meaning "top of the mountains." As the first transcontinental railroad came to completion, it was apparent that Utah would become the crossroads of the West. As rail development expanded across the United States, Ogden became the main junction for trains from the Northwest, Southwest and West Coast as a funnel to the East. The discovery of copper, iron ore, silver, gold, and coal in Utah drove the rails to the mining areas of the state for export to other areas of the United States as well as overseas. As time went on, traffic levels grew to great proportions. However, the barrier of the Wasatch Range proved a great problem, forcing the railroads that crossed it to use extremely large locomotives, many of them holding the title as "World's Largest."

This book covers this history from 1869 to the present. It covers the historical significance the railroads played in the development of Utah as well as in the growth of the United States. The Ogden Union Station Foundation commissioned me to do 20 paintings to illustrate the growth of railroads in the state. The renderings in this book take the different pieces of motive power and rolling stock found at the museum, and depict them as they were used in daily service. Hence, to be historically accurate, some discrepancies, exist between how the subject matter appears in the paintings as opposed to how they are currently preserved.

I have illustrated both the motive power, rolling stock, and scenes as accurately as possible. I have counted the rivets, nuts, and bolts and made sure that all the detail is present. I admit some of the paintings were more enjoyable to do than others, as I prefer to do large steam locomotives over just about anything else.

Doing a book of this nature has been a dream of mine ever since I learned which end of a brush to put the paint on. In a way I am glad that no other museums took me up on this idea as, being a Utah native, it is only right that I do my state first.

In discussions with the Foundation about the book, we found that many of the initial ideas had to be changed or eliminated to come up with the final paintings in this book. My many meetings with Robert Geier and Dr. Stephen Carr helped to refine my ideas for the images that follow. I give them many thanks as this book would not have been possible without them.

The original paintings in this book are done in watercolor and in oil. The watercolor is done on watercolor board, and the oils on linen. The palette I use for both oil and watercolor use the same 15 colors. They are white, yellow ochre, indian yellow, alizarin crimson, light and medium cadmium red, ultramarine blue, prussian blue, thalo blue, thalo green, green earth hue, sap green, raw umber, burnt sienna and paynes gray. The originals are on display as part of the rail history exhibit at Ogden Union Station.

I have been interested in trains as long as I can remember. I guess that interest came from my dad, to whom this book is dedicated. Somewhere in my youth was unleashed a talent that was God-given but neglected until I took a beginning oil painting class while pursuing an architectural degree at the University of Utah. It's all history after that.

I must also thank my wife, Gayleen, for her patience while the paintings for this book were completed. And additional thanks to clients who have had to wait for their paintings until the paintings for this book were complete.

I have had many enjoyable hours doing the paintings. I hope those who read the text and study the paintings will find many enjoyable hours as well.

– *Gilbert H. Bennett*

— Legend for Map Locations —

1   Promontory
Completion of the first Transcontinental Railroad.

2   Desert
Rio Grande Western's 3-foot mainline between Salt Lake City, Utah, and Denver, Colorado, standard-gauged in 1891 and merged into the Denver & Rio Grande Western Railroad; now owned by Union Pacific.

3   Tintic Mining District
San Pedro, Los Angeles & Salt Lake Railroad access to Eureka, Mammoth and Silver City.

4, 12   Ogden
Union Station of the Union Pacific, Central Pacific-Southern Pacific, Denver & Rio Grande Western; Bamberger Lines; Utah Idaho Central.

5   Salt Lake City
Union Station of the Denver & Rio Grande Western and the Western Pacific.

6   Low
Western Pacific's crossing of the Cedar Mountains in the western Utah desert.

7   Covered Bridge
Denver & Rio Grande Western's mainline over Soldier Summit.

8   Hyrum
Utah Idaho Central's line between Ogden, Utah, and Preston, Idaho.

9   Wanship
Union Pacific's line to Park City.

10   Lake Point
San Pedro, Los Angles & Salt Lake's mainline between Salt Lake City, Utah, and Los Angeles, California.

11   Gateway
Union Pacific's transcontinental mainline over the Wasatch Mountains. The line was double-tracked between 1916-23.

13   Ogden
Union Pacific's Ogden roundhouse.

14   MidLake
Southern Pacific's Lucin Cutoff across the Great Salt Lake.

15   Taggart
Union Pacific's east- west mainline.

16   Emory
Union Pacific's mainline over the Wasatch.

17   Castle Gate
Utah Railway's and the Denver & Rio Grande Western's mainline in the Price River canyon over the Wasatch.

18   Yale
San Pedro, Los Angeles & Salt Lake's mainline through the southwestern Utah desert.

19   Scenic
Denver & Rio Grande Western's new 2 percent grade built to replace the 4 percent grade on Soldier Summit in 1912.

20   Echo
Union Pacific's mainline up Echo canyon in northeastern Utah.

— Map Legend —
(Continued)

The numbers in the Legend, which refer to the locations on the Utah map where the paintings in the book were depicted as having taken place, also correspond to the chapters in the book. Inasmuch as each painting represents a single chapter, done in chronological order starting with 1869, the numbers of necessity appear to be placed randomly on the map.

Railroad abbreviations

CP - Central Pacific
D&RGW - Denver Rio Grande Western
SP - Southern Pacific
SP,LA&SL - San Pedro, Los Angeles & Salt Lake
UIC - Utah Idaho Central
UP - Union Pacific
URY - Utah Railway
WP - Western Pacific

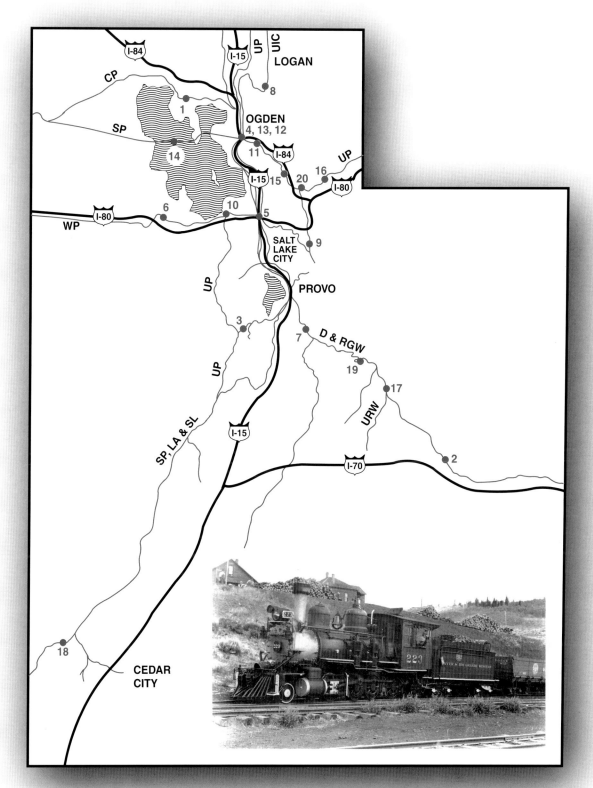

Chapter 1

"Done!"

Central Pacific and Union Pacific at Promontory
May 10, 1869

May 10, 1869. One of the most important dates in Utah history and in the history of American railroading: the completion of the first transcontinental railroad.

In 1862, President Abraham Lincoln signed the Pacific Railroad Act which authorized the construction of two railroads, the Union Pacific westward from Council Bluffs, Iowa; and the Central Pacific, eastward from Sacramento, California, toward each other to a meeting point. Begun in 1865, using light locomotives and rather primitive construction methods, the construction companies forged ahead through the best grades that the various terrains had to offer.

The Central Pacific had the most difficult task, building a rail line up a generally steady 2 percent grade almost immediately after leaving Sacramento. This required heavy drilling and blasting of numerous tunnels through the hard granite rock in the Sierra Nevada Mountains. It took two and a half years just to construct over this one mountain range. Even then, the company had to build 23 miles of snowsheds to be able to operate in the winter when often 40 feet of snow would cover the tracks. However, once the railroad reached Reno, Nevada, it was practically level across the Great Basin and construction proceeded much faster.

The Union Pacific had a much easier time to start with. The countryside from Omaha, Nebraska, to Cheyenne, Wyoming, is essentially flat, just an almost imperceptible rise from east to west. Several large rivers required bridging, but only four tunnels needed to be drilled, one in Wyoming and three in Utah. But extra time was required to build the section down through Echo and Weber Canyons. Grenville Dodge, Chief Engineer for the Union Pacific, stated that it cost more money per mile to build down through these canyons than anywhere else on the road. Even then, though, Union Pacific was able to construct more miles by far than the Central Pacific.

As the distance between the two construction teams shortened, it became apparent that the meeting place would likely be somewhere in northern Utah Territory. The U.S. Congress had failed to specify a meeting point in the original Act, and even in the Second Act of 1864, so the two construction companies built roadbed grades far in advance of the actual laying of ties and rails, resulting in parallel grades built by the two outfits for almost 200 miles through northern Utah. And the contractors were being paid by the construction of miles of railroad whether there were rails laid on or not. Finally, Congress specified that the meeting point would be at the desolate location known as Promontory Summit. (Please do not confuse this location with Promontory Point. That is a completely different spot and has no connection with the construction of the Transcontinental Railroad. Aside from the obscure note where early surveyors were considering crossing the Great Salt Lake's Bear River Bay directly west from Ogden to the Point, no mention is made to this Point in the railroad's construction. See chapter 14 to learn how the Southern Pacific eventually did lay track to the Point.)

By the time the rail lines reached Promontory, the members of the track gangs were working so well together that they were able to lay many more miles of track in a day than had ever been done before. Just a few days before the final completion, the Central Pacific rail crews laid 10 miles of track in one day — a feat that has never been equaled using strictly human power.

The entire nation was awaiting the final event, the driving of the last spike, there were two aspects to the ceremony. First, a polished, commemorative laurelwood tie from California was placed under the two rails, with holes already pre-drilled to accept the ceremonial spikes of which there were four. The final spike, crafted of high-grade gold alloy, also from California, was dropped into its hole. When the speech-making was concluded, the commanding officer of the army unit present tapped the head of the golden spike several times with the hilt of his saber. Then the spikes and laurel tie were removed. (Although the wooden tie was destroyed during the 1906 San Francisco fire, the final golden spike, complete with dents in the head from the officer's saber taps, is still on display in the library of the Stanford University in Palo Alto, California.)

Second, a regular railroad tie was inserted in place under the rails, and three iron spikes were driven in to secure the rails to the tie. Then the last spike was wired up to the telegrapher's table, as was the spike maul, so that when the two iron objects came together the nation's citizenry would know that the country was indeed united by steel. In actuality, this idea didn't work. As the first principal of the ceremony, Governor Leland Stanford of the Central Pacific, swung the maul he missed the spike. Thomas Durant, Vice-President of the Union Pacific, then swung the maul, and in deference to Governor Stanford, also missed. The nearby telegraph operator took matters into his own hands and tapped his key as if the maul and spike had made contact. It finally fell to the two railroads' respective general superintendents, J.H. Strobridge of the C.P and Samuel Reed of the U.P. to actually drive in the last spike.

So in actuality the golden spike was not the "last" spike driven, but was strictly symbolic and commemorative. The "last" spike was an ordinary one pulled from the spike keg and hammered into place. However, as it turned out, there were quite a number of "final" spikes, no one really knows how many. Because, as soon as the "last" spike was driven in, the final speeches were made, the locomotives were rolled over the meeting point and finally everyone had dispersed, the souvenir hunters descended on the "last" spike and yanked it from the tie. Within a short time, all four last spikes had been extracted from the tie, and the wooden tie itself had been hacked apart by knives and hatchets and carted away in pieces.

During the next few days, the "last" tie had to be replaced half a dozen times and a whole kegful of "last" spikes were used before those who gathered souvenirs were satisfied and eventually left the spot alone.

Today, the Golden Spike National Historic Site is administered by the National Park Service. Rails have been re-laid on the original rail beds and replicas of the original locomotives, Central Pacific's #60, *Jupiter,* and Union Pacific's #119, painstakingly researched as to the original color schemes, and complete down to the last rivet, can be seen daily during the summer tourist season. Re-enactment scenes and ceremonies, as depicted in the painting, are put on around May 10th of each year and again during Railroad Days, usually in September.

"DONE!"

Oil 22" x 28" 1997

When Bob Geier and I met together to go over the images for this book, it was clear that a painting of the completion of the first transcontinental railroad would be a must. I admit that at first I was excited over the challenge of doing the research and layout of the painting. However, everything soon ground to a halt as trying to find good photos of what I had in my mind just couldn't be found.

I had envisioned doing the May 10th extravaganza from the Central Pacific or west side of Promontory Summit. I had envisioned the snow-capped peaks of the Wasatch off in the distance plus a hint of the Great Salt Lake along the right edge of the painting. As the sketching started I began running into problems. From that vantage point, the lake would not be seen nor would the snow-capped Wasatch range. It was back to the drawing board.

I was once again talking with Bob at the celebration of the 100th year of Utah Statehood when an unknown gentleman overheard us and suggested I do the painting based on the one that Howard Fogg had done for the Union Pacific back in 1968. He also stated that the painting was done incorrectly and that it would be nice to see it done right. I had previously thought about using the Fogg painting as a base as well as using other paintings, but I found all the renditions to be historically incorrect.

To assure historic accuracy, I went to the library and read the first hand accounts of those who attended the celebration as well as historians' compilations of the events that occurred that day. I also dug out the builder's plans for both the *Jupiter* and #119.

May 10, 1869, was a cold day for May. The wind off the Great Salt Lake added to the chill as people and dignitaries from the Territory of Utah and surrounding states, as well as the railroads, all joined together. I checked the A. J. Russell and Charles R. Savage photos of the building of the transcontinental to glean more information. I knew that with a crowd of people the locomotives would be difficult to see, so the view had to be elevated. Wagons, tents and horses for 500 people as well as those that had built the railroad had to be in view also. Using artist license, I eliminated about 500 wagons and carriages by moving to the east side of the summit.

As the painting started to unfold, the cold blue sky, the barren Promontory range and the action of the event just fell in place. The designs on the tender of #119 were taken from an 1869 photograph taken in Weber Canyon. The colors of the locomotives and tenders are as accurate as possible albeit a little more clean than they would have been all those years ago. I wish I could have witnessed this event myself. However, doing this painting is probably as close as I will ever get.

Do I like the end result? Yes!

Chapter 2

Slim Rails and Sagebrush

Rio Grande Western in Eastern Utah
1889

At one time, in the late 1880's, Utah stood right in the center of a three-foot narrow-gauged railroad system that stretched some 1250 miles from Denver, Colorado, through Salt Lake City and Ogden, through Pocatello and Idaho Falls, Idaho to Butte and Garrison, Montana.

William Jackson Palmer, in the 1870's, was trying to construct a rail line from Denver, Colorado, to Santa Fe, New Mexico Territory, and possibly all the way to Mexico as trade routes were being established between our two countries. However, he became thwarted when attempting to cross over Raton Pass, just across the Colorado line, because the Santa Fe Railway had reached there first. The courts agreed with Santa Fe's position, and Palmer and his Denver & Rio Grande Railway had to look elsewhere. Fortunately, elsewhere was to be had. Just about that time, numerous silver strikes had been discovered in the midst of the Rocky Mountains in central Colorado, mines were being developed, and transportation was needed to get the ore to the mills and smelters.

Palmer then turned his interests westward and built his three-foot narrow gauge railroad up to the mines in various locations. Eventually, narrow-gauged rails roamed through the Rockies to the western flanks of the mountains. Transcontinental fever was raging at that time, and the D&RG decided to build all the way to California. A new company, the Denver & Rio Grande Western Railway, was organized and proceeded across the Colorado state/ Utah Territory line. The economics of the times began to catch up with the proposal, however, and instead of continuing along the survey routes through central Utah, thence to the Los Angeles basin, the company turned the survey and construction forces north-westerly toward the rapidly growing Salt Lake Valley. The citizens of Salt Lake City and numerous nearby towns and villages were happy to encourage this new railroad so as to provide competition to the only other outside rail line in the area, the all-powerful Union Pacific.

The new railway bought up several small narrow gauge lines in Salt Lake and Utah valleys, which helped shorten the time of construction. Included was the Utah & Pleasant Valley, which already ran from Springville, over Soldier Summit, down to Tucker and up to Pleasant Valley.

Narrow-gauged railroad construction is generally faster, cheaper and a lot more forgiving than that of the standard gauge of four feet eight-and-a-half inches between the rails. Curves can be made sharper for the shorter engines and cars, and grades can be allowed to be a little steeper. Construction of this railroad proceeded from the ends, i.e., the Utah boundary and Salt Lake City, toward some point in between. The rolling badlands of the eastern Utah desert were crossed with a minimum of effort — lots of curves but very little in the way of grades. The Price River

Canyon was utilized, many miles east of Price, which necessitated the bridging of the river several times and the drilling of the only narrow gauge tunnel in Utah. The final meeting point of the two construction companies was at an isolated spot in the eastern desert called Desert Siding. After modest ceremonies, trains started running between Salt Lake City and Denver.

The narrow-gauged line eventually was extended north to Ogden. It was then possible to ride from Denver to Grand Junction on the D&RG Railway, then to Ogden on the D&RGW Railway and on to Butte, Montana, on the Oregon Short Line & Utah Northern — all on three-foot narrow-gauged trackage.

By the late 1880's, however, it became apparent to all involved in railroading, manufacturing and shipping that the three-foot narrow gauge would not be satisfactory for mainline operations due to size constraints and the enormous difficulties in exchanging goods between railroads of different gauges. In 1890, the D&RGW Railway was reorganized into the Rio Grande Western Railway and working with the D&RG Railway in Colorado, the entire mainline between Ogden and Denver was expanded to standard gauge. (The lines north of Ogden were also standard-gauged by the Union Pacific, which by then had taken control of the OSL &UN.) In most places along the route, this meant simply widening the gauge of the existing track, in some cases installing longer ties. Several locations in eastern Utah, though, were deemed inadequate for that procedure, so several miles of completely new roadbed and trackage were built along part of the Colorado River, replacing the curving mainline west of the Colorado line. The twisting, flood-prone Price River Canyon was also abandoned in favor of a new,

straighter route a couple of miles farther north — the present alignment of the railroad.

The painting depicts diminutive locomotive #223 pulling a mixed train (part freight-part passenger) eastbound along the foothills of the Book Cliffs in eastern Utah about 1889, a year before standard-gauging. This narrow gauge train has left the tight confines of Price River canyon behind and is heading toward the badlands just west of the Colorado-Utah border, then to Grand Junction where a new train crew will take over.

Engine #223 was built by the Grant Locomotive Works in 1881, and operated in eastern Utah and western Colorado from 1881 until 1890. It was then used on some narrow gauge lines in southwestern Colorado that were never standard-gauged. In July 1941, the locomotive was presented to Salt Lake City by the Denver & Rio Grande Western Railroad (successor to the Rio Grande Western Railway, the Denver & Rio Grande Railway, and the Denver & Rio Grande Western Railway). It reposed in Liberty Park in Salt Lake City until the 1970's when it was moved to the trackside platform of the Rio Grande depot.

In 1995 the city deeded it over to the Utah State Railroad Museum at the Ogden Union Station where it is undergoing restoration. Because of extensive dry-rotting of the oak timbers of the tender frame and the rusting of many metal parts of the century-plus old machine, much rebuilding and restoring will be needed to make this delightful little 2-8-0 Consolidation-type engine presentable. Working from some original mechanical drawings, the restorationists will preserve as much as possible of the engine and rebuild other parts that are too rusted to be of use.

SLIM RAILS AND SAGEBRUSH

Oil 18" x 24" 1997

The first steam locomotive I saw as a child was #223. My father used to take the family to Liberty Park in Salt Lake City, to ride the merry-go-round and Ferris wheel. I used to wander off to go see the big (to a four-year-old) steam locomotive. I could stare at this marvelous machine for hours wondering how it would have been to see this locomotive run. Deep down it has always been one of my favorites.

During the 1970's #223 was moved to the back of the Denver & Rio Grande Western depot where it was vandalized and neglected. I was sad to see what was happening to this locomotive. Years later I was asked to be on an informal group to save #223. The narrow gauge tourist lines in Colorado wanted the locomotive refurbished to running condition for use with special trains and movies. Although the locomotive would be gone from Utah, it would meet a much better fate than sitting behind the depot in neglect.

The locomotive finally ended up in Ogden where it will be restored to cosmetic if not running condition. I look forward to when this little locomotive will again be turned back to the condition it was when I was a child

As #223 now resides at the Utah State Railroad Museum, I agreed to do a painting of it. My idea was to put it in its 1930's dress (as it will be restored in) running up the Baldwin branch in western Colorado. Bob had other ideas. He wanted to know if the locomotive could be rendered running somewhere in Utah. My first sketch was of #223 in 1890's dress at the old Ogden depot. While I am sure the locomotive ran in Utah it would not have come that far west. Again the library came in handy.

Locomotive #223 is a C-16 built in 1881 by Grant Locomotive Works. The "C" stands for Consolidation, a 2-8-0 wheel arrangement with 16,000 pounds of tractive effort. (See page 93 for further explanations of wheel arrangements and numbers). The locomotive was stationed mainly on the western part of the Denver & Rio Grande. As the Denver & Rio Grande and the Rio Grande Western's traffic levels fluctuated, locomotives where borrowed from one railroad to the other to ease the motive power crunch, hence the excuse for #223 to be in Utah.

I had always wanted to do this painting with a D&RGW L-105 4-6-6-4 in snow with the Book Cliffs behind. However, to make this painting different, I chose a hot summer afternoon with a mixed passenger train going east. I believe this to be accurate down to the Grant builder's plate! As I look at the painting, I see that not much has changed in the area in the past 108 years; only the track has been widened and a freeway put in, other than that it's the same arid land as it was when the first rails were laid there.

This is one of my favorite paintings in the book. Still I wonder when I will be able to do that 4-6-6-4 running across this same area under dark winter skies.

Chapter 3

Mines, Mountains and Sidewinders

San Pedro, Los Angeles & Salt Lake Railroad near Eureka, Utah
1910

One of the more unusual types of steam locomotives was the geared type where the steam cylinders, instead of operating reciprocal pistons as on the standard steam engine, turned a crankshaft attached to gears which propelled the locomotive. There were three main geared types, with a smattering of others built by localized machine companies or by railroads themselves. They were all constructed for use on lightweight, uneven track, sharp curves, and steep grades typical of mining and lumbering areas. Because of the gear ratios, they were generally not designed to travel more than about 10 to 15 miles per hour, but due to the gears these engines could pull a heavier than usual train on the mountain grades they had to encounter.

The Climax type was built by the Climax Manufacturing Company in Corry, Pennsylvania. This engine was built with two cylinders, one on each side, but higher up on the side and sloping down backward. The piston rods connected with a jack shaft, which operated the main drive shaft under the engine, which turned gears between the wheels of the two power trucks.

The Heisler type was originally constructed by the Stearns Manufacturing Company in Erie, Pennsylvania, in 1894, later to be known as the Heisler Locomotive Works. This locomotive had a cylinder on each side of the boiler with the piston rods pointing downward under the boiler like the letter 'V'. The rods connected with gearing, which drove the under-boiler shaft to the trucks.

Ephraim Shay invented the locomotive type portrayed in the painting. It was named after him and was produced by the Lima Machine Works in Lima, Ohio, starting in 1880. This company after 1901 went on to become one of the three major steam locomotive builders in the nation. An unusual feature of the Shay engine is that the boiler is not centered on the frame but is positioned on the left side. This is to accommodate the three (occasionally two) vertical cylinders that are situated above the rail under the right side. The three cylinders operate off the steam from the boiler similar to a standard steam engine, but are connected to a crankshaft, similar to an automobile crankshaft The shaft then turns a set of gears on the two right-hand wheels of each truck. Smaller Shays used the two trucks under the locomotive to power the engine. Larger engines, such as the one pictured, also had a continuation of the shaft to a third power truck under the tender. The weight of the tender, especially when full of fuel and water, added to the traction of the third truck and produced additional power to help the two locomotive trucks. On level track, this engine could reach a speed of 20 miles per hour, but was almost never run more than 15 miles per hour and usually much slower. This type was known to negotiate grades as steep as 14 percent, and 8-10 percent grades were not at all unusual. Because of the numerous moving parts, mainly situated close to the bottom of the engine where dirt, dust, and accumulated debris could interfere with operation, these engines required a lot more maintenance than most regular steam engines. With all the steel meshing together, even when properly lubricated, the noise produced by these engines was so unusually loud that many a railroader jumped clear of a track when he heard the noise coming at him, yet the locomotive might not show up for several minutes.

Utah's mining boom began in 1863, long after similar booms in surrounding states or territories. Gold was discovered in Bingham Canyon, then later at Mercur. Silver and associated metals such as lead and zinc were located in a number of areas, notably Alta, Park City, Ophir, the Tintic area, Frisco, and Newhouse areas and even at Silver Reef at the bottom of the state. Silver Reef was situated too far away from a railroad and was never served by one, but all the others eventually had rail lines built into them. Because hard-rock mining occurred mostly in mountainous terrain, it was natural that several of these mining railroads would utilize some of the geared locomotives.

The only Climax locomotives known to be used in Utah were the two that belonged to the St. John & Ophir Railroad, which ran from St. John Station on Union Pacific's Los Angeles & Salt Lake line up to Ophir Canyon, then on the 7 percent grade up to the mining town of Ophir. This railroad ran from 1912 until 1928.

Sidewinding Shay locomotives were found in a variety of locations. The Copper Belt Railroad had at least two in the upper reaches of Bingham Canyon on 7.4 percent grades around 1900. The Newhouse, Copper Gulch & Sevier Lake Railroad owned one in the desert mountains east of Newhouse between 1904 and 1909. The Salt Lake & Mercur Railroad, running from the Fairfield Station

up over the Oquirrh Mountains into Mercur, owned six Shays beginning as early as 1895. The New East Tintic Railroad, a two-mile long road built in 1897 from the Oregon Short Line at Mammoth in the Tintic District, up to the Mammoth Mine, also owned two standard-gauged Shays. This tiny rail line, along with its locomotives, was absorbed into the San Pedro, Los Angeles & Salt Lake Railroad. These were two of the only three Shay locomotives owned by the Union Pacific. They spent the rest of their useful lives working around the Eureka and Mammoth areas of the Tintic Mining District.

Several three-foot narrow gauge Shays were known to operate in Utah. One ran on the Eureka Hill Railroad from Silver City up into the mountains northward. The Salt Lake & Feet Douglas Railway's ran from downtown Salt Lake City up to Feet Douglas and to the mouth of Emigration Canyon. The Little Cottonwood Transportation Company operated four of these engines between Granite, at the mouth of Little Cottonwood Canyon, in Salt Lake County, up to the mines at Alta. An even smaller Shay, running on 30-inch gauge, was utilized on the Crescent Tramway from Park City up to the Crescent Mine high in the mountains southwest of town.

No examples of the Heisler geared locomotive were known to have operated in Utah.

The painting shows one of the Tintic Shays pushing a load of empty gondolas up toward Eureka. The grade here is moderate, but farther up in town it reaches 7 percent. The Tintic Range Railway, subsequently merged into the D&RGW system, was built into Eureka in 1891 from the east; its track can be seen on the right side of the painting.

MINES, MOUNTAINS AND SIDEWINDERS

Watercolor 18" x 24" 1997

The Tintic mining area has always been one of my favorite locations. Old timber mine heads still dot the landscapes of narrow canyons. When Bob told me he wanted some of the mining areas in Utah to be in the book, I knew exactly what I wanted to paint: the Tintic district.

The Tintic mining area consisted of the towns of Eureka, Silver City, and Mammoth, located in the East Tintic Mountains. These towns had boom and bust cycles as did most mining towns. Almost overnight the population of the towns exploded. The railroads, following the money and people, also tapped into the areas. The San Pedro, Los Angeles & Salt Lake Railroad ran its line from Tintic Junction up to Eureka from the west. The Denver & Rio Grande Western came in from the east. The grades for both railroads were steep and winding. The D&RGW used small mallet locomotives while the SP, LA & SL opted to use Shay locomotives.

The Shay locomotive was invented by Ephraim Shay of the Lima Locomotive works. The locomotive was built for light rail, steep grades, and sharp curves. Three cylinders mounted vertically turned a drive shaft that powered gear-driven trucks (the powered wheels under diesel electric, electric and gear-driven locomotives). Though many railroads that used Shays in the state, the most famous and photographed were numbers 59 and 61 used in the Tintic mining district.

I chose to render #60. This locomotive was the least photographed of the three Shays used on the line, due to its being scrapped in 1916. I wanted a view that was not the usual wedge shot from the front, hence I used the Shay from the rear. The locomotive is shoving an empty set of cars to be loaded with ore to be taken to the smelters in the Salt Lake City area. The location is just coming into Eureka with the outer homes and some of the mine heads and buildings that are now gone. The area around Eureka is high and dry. I struggled to get the correct color of the arid soil. To be honest, my two year old son came up with the right color combination. I took a break. Okay, I wanted a donut! I left just for a few seconds to go to the kitchen. When I came back, there was my two year old son playing artist with my paints and brushes. He had a great big smile and said "Look, daddy"! At that time a million things went through my mind. Among them fear, panic and putting a two year old up for adoption. However, as I looked closer he had mixed the color I had tried to get all that morning. I bribed him away from the painting with my donut and continued to finish the scenery he had started.

This is the only painting in the book of a steam locomotive done in watercolor. To me it would have worked in either oil or watercolor. Someday I would like to do this painting in oil just to see the difference of the two side-by-side. Any takers?

Chapter 4

Summer's Eve

Ogden Union Station
1917

With the exception of cities built on the banks of rivers, most large American cities were built around a major railroad station. Very often the depot became the largest building in town and frequently the focal point of the city's development. Such was the case at Ogden, even though Ogden might be considered one of the smallest "major" cities in the nation. Even then, the beginning of Ogden's railroad architecture was anything but auspicious.

By 1874, four railroad companies existed in the city between the west edge of town, Wall Avenue, and the Weber River. Union Pacific, Central Pacific, Utah Central and Utah Northern each had its own locomotive facilities and depot. Finally, in 1878, due to increasing traffic, with at least 16 trains per day, a common depot building was decided upon — the wooden Union Pacific station. Erected in 1869, it was small, gloomy, dark, and unbefitting for the "modern" passenger traffic that was then being observed daily. In addition, the wooden sidewalks running between the station tracks and around the depot were muddy and unkempt. For the next eight years, passengers and the general public complained about how unattractive the station area was, especially considering that it was the entrance to the city for most travelers of the day.

In 1886, the president of Union Pacific, the dominant railroad, authorized the construction of a new union depot. Designed by Kansas City architect Henry Van Brundt, it was to be built in the Romanesque style as were several other buildings being constructed during the period, such as the Salt Lake City and County building. And if the Ogden Union Depot is somewhat similar to stations built in Omaha, Nebraska, Cheyenne, Wyoming, and Portland, Oregon, it is because they were also designed by Van Brundt, as commissioned by Union Pacific.

In 1888, about the time Union Pacific was taking over the Utah Central and the Utah & Northern, the U.P. and Central Pacific organized the Ogden Union Railway & Depot Company. This company correlated all rail activity, passenger, and freight, into and through the city, and helped to finance the construction of the depot and other improvements in the area.

The new depot was completed in July 1889 and was some 374 feet long by about 88 feet wide with a central clock tower. Railroad offices were in the upper floor of the central area, with ticket offices and waiting rooms below. The north wing was a huge baggage handling area and an emigrant waiting room. The south wing comprised a 33-room hotel. This depot then became the focal point and most notable aspect of town. The impressive building showed that Ogden was a major junction city despite having a population of only around 12,000.

Rail traffic continued to increase yearly providing much employment for each of the railroads, which now also included the Rio Grande, the Ogden, Logan & Idaho (later known as the

Utah Idaho Central) and the Salt Lake & Ogden (later, the Bamberger). Rail traffic also helped Ogden become not only one of the three or four largest rail centers between the Missouri River and the Pacific Coast, but also brought in numerous canneries, factories, machine shops, clothing mills, warehouse companies, and brick and lumber yards. By 1915, the depot was handling 76 passenger trains a day. Numerous through trains ran on Union Pacific and Southern Pacific, with the D&RGW bringing three a day either to hand off to the Southern Pacific across the Lucin Cutoff or to Union Pacific bound for the Pacific Northwest. Southern Pacific also ran a local accommodation out to Kelton, west of Promontory and north of the Great Salt Lake on the all but abandoned original transcontinental line. Union Pacific operated several trains a day between Ogden and Pocatello as well as a local from Salt Lake City to Cache Junction.

Keeping up with the passenger activity was the tremendous surge of freight traffic. The Union Railway & Depot was required to switch hundreds of cars a day from incoming trains on all railroads to blocks of cars destined for other railways and destinations. A new icehouse was built that eventually could service 272 cars in one hour. Well over a thousand men were employed in the various roundhouses, freight stations, the ice house, railroad warehouses and the Union Station, not to mention many hundreds of engine and train crews that used Ogden as a terminal or division point and crew change location. In 1917, the completion of the Ogden Union Stockyards made the city the largest city west of Denver in handling livestock in railroad stock cars. The year 1921 became the peak year for Union Pacific passenger revenues at the station.

Then in the midst of all this prosperity, tragedy fell. On February 13, 1923, one of the station hotel rooms caught fire and within a few hours the entire center section of the depot had been destroyed, taking with it all of the railroads' controls and equipment. Although the north wing and most of the south wing were spared, the imposing center section was just a shell of stone. Surprisingly, no one was injured or killed, with the exception of a railroad clerk, killed several days later when he was struck on the head by a stone falling from the ruined clock tower. Also, somewhat surprising, was the reaction from most of the local citizens. Despite its imposing appearance, the depot was considered poorly lighted, not ventilated well, dour-appearing and generally unattractive. Everyone expected the railroads to immediately plan for a new building. Although initially the railroads desired to reconstruct the old design, pressure from the populace resulted in a brand-new Union Station that used the same foundation stones as the old one. This time, however, the style was of the Italian Renaissance with a Spanish tile roof. Similar stations are to be found at Milford, Utah, Caliente, Nevada, and Kelso, California.

The painting shows the track side of the original depot in 1917, during the peak years of passenger travel through Ogden. As in the later World War, the first World War produced much rail traffic, both in freight and war materiel, and in transporting soldiers by the tens of thousands through Union Station. While a new train crew gets its orders, servicemen from the last car of a nameless passenger train or possibly troop train visit the USO table for a bit of refreshment.

SUMMER'S EVE

Watercolor 18" x 24" 1997

A few years ago I was in Albuquerque, New Mexico, photographing the station as Amtrak's *Southwest Chief* arrived. On the platform, toward the front of the train, was a table tended by two, let's just say elderly, women. Two men in uniform walked to the table and the ladies started conversing with them. The ladies gave them a sandwich wrapped in cellophane, a doughnut and some coffee. After the train departed, I spoke with the two women and found that they were Red Cross volunteers who met the train every day to serve servicemen free food.

I knew that a rendering of the old Ogden depot had to be in the book. The first idea was of #223 with a passenger train in back of the station. It would be afternoon or early evening with long shadows and the activity of a train ready to depart. The painting for #223 took on its own life leaving me with a "what to do" with the depot? As I looked at the sketch I had drawn, I still wanted to capture the feeling and stillness of a late summer's day. I wanted some action but nothing overbearing. This meant no locomotives but maybe a train car or two and a few people milling about. I believe it was Dr. Carr who came up with the idea of doing a troop train in the station during World War I.

As I set up the painting, I could see it was going to be too still.

I needed something to balance the weight of the clock tower that would fit in the lower right side of the painting. Many things came to mind, none of them good, when the images from my journey to Albuquerque came flooding back. I did some research and came up with a few troop trains, some period signs and bunting on the station. On the platform, I put that table with white linen and those silver pitchers of coffee I had remembered from Albuquerque. Most of the soldiers of that time would have just been 18 to 22 years of age. Free food no matter how good or bad would naturally cause a line. The painting all came together. Doughboys (the foot soldiers) and sailors talk with one another perhaps discussing where they are going, perhaps remembering where they have been. I guess as one looks at this painting one may come up with his own stories. Are the servicemen going home? Are they headed across country to go overseas? This scene happened countless times in stations all across America. My hat is off to the men who fought to uphold our freedom, and to the railroads that moved staggering amounts of goods to support them.

In this painting, though the war is far away, there is peace and warmth at the station this summer's eve in Ogden.

Chapter 5

Quiet Village
Salt Lake City Union Station
1922

What is a decent-sized American city without its Union Station? Passengers coming and going through depots at all times of the day and night could almost always be assured of having available facilities , a shoe stand and a counter to pick up a snack or a full meal.

Actually, the term "Union Station" referred to a depot handling the passengers of two or more railroads. Most of the grandiose depots of the storied past were union stations serving the multitudes in cities such as New York, Chicago, St. Louis and Kansas City. As the railroads spread to the West, fewer cities were served by more than one rail line, and then often each railway would have its own station rather than sharing space with another.

Salt Lake City was a bit unusual back in the heydays of passenger service. Although only three mainline roads entered the city, two of them, the Denver & Rio Grande Western and the Western Pacific used the same facilities, such as depot, yard and engine servicing areas. So, even though the two railroads terminated in Salt Lake, one from the East, the other from the West, because they both used the depot it was a "union station."

A complicating feature, however, was the station of the other major railroad just three blocks to the north—the Union Pacific. Union Pacific was the dominating railway in the city, operating several more daily trains than either of the other two combined, so naturally its depot was much more active. Thus, when a person would say he/she was going to Union Station, another may not always be certain which station was being referred to—Union Station or Union Pacific station.

The original Salt Lake D&RGW depot was constructed at 2nd South and Fifth (now Sixth) West streets. Built around 1882, when the railroad was a narrow gauge line, it was a large, attractive two-and-a-half story structure, essentially the western terminus of the Rio Grande, although a few trains continued north to Ogden. Early photos show the three-foot gauge tracks and stub switches common to that era.

In 1910, to coincide with the completion of the Western Pacific from Salt Lake to Oakland, California, the two railroads formed the Salt Lake City Union Depot Company for train switching purposes and constructed the present Union Station building at the bottom of Third South (Broadway) and Rio Grande Street (455 West). The building was designed by Henry Schlacks, noted Chicago architect, in the Beaux Arts Classical-Renaissance Revival style.

At the same time as the construction of Union Station, Union Pacific's president, E. H. Harriman, had purchased the rag-tag Salt Lake City streetcar system and was in the process of developing it into the finest, for the time, street railway operation in the country, the Utah Light & Railway Company.

Even with a population of barely 15,000 in 1872, city planners felt that there was a need for a streetcar system. From then until 1889, the cars were pulled by mules. Successful systems had been recently built in other cities using newly discovered and usable electricity. The Salt Lake City Railroad then converted to electrical power and sent the mules out to pasture. Competing streetcar lines soon sprang up, such as the Salt Lake Rapid Transit, the Popperton Place & Fort Douglas Rapid Transit, the East Bench Street Railway Company, and later the West Side Rapid Transit. In 1901, all these except for the West Side line were merged with the Salt Lake City Railroad into the Consolidated Railway & Power Company which operated over 80 miles of track, much of it double-trackage down many of the city's wide streets.

In 1904, the Consolidated Railway was merged with the Utah Light and Power Company forming the Utah Light & Railway. Under Harriman, new lines were built, and others extended as far south as Sandy, southeast to Holladay, and north to Centerville in Davis County. New, heavy rail was installed and practically the entire system was double-tracked with the exception of the lines to the outlying suburbs. New carbarns, shops, and rebuilding facilities were constructed at Fifth South and Seventh East streets. By 1913, the trolley system was the envy of many cities much larger than Salt Lake City. Dozens of streetcar and city planners from all over the western hemisphere visited the Salt Lake Valley to see this storied operation.

By 1914 Harriman had died and the company was reorganized into the Utah Light & Traction Company, which lasted until the end of the streetcar operation. The trolley business was brisk and needed for decades until it became apparent that the versatility of buses outweighed the continued cost of electric street railway maintenance. Two-pole trolley buses then made their appearance (the first such operation in the United States), to then be replaced by gasoline buses. The end of World War II signalled the resurgence of the auto industry and soon most families owned cars. The last trolley line was finally shut down in 1944.

Like most cities around the nation where streetcar lines were built to the most prominent train stations, Salt Lake City's lines were directed to the front entrances of both the Union Pacific and Union stations to handle the myriad of passengers coming and going. In the 1920's, typified by the painting of Salt Lake's Union Station, not only did the Western Pacific have four daily trains arriving and departing, the Rio Grande had 20. Besides the mainline trains between Salt Lake and Denver, there were run-through schedules to Ogden, plus other accommodations between Salt Lake and Park City, Heber City, Bingham Canyon, Richfield and Marysvale. In addition, the Union Pacific depot handled dozens of trains per day.

The only things left from the trolley era, besides numerous miles of track still buried beneath many of the downtown streets, are the few streetcars situated as props around the mall at Trolley Square, the renovated carbarns of the former day.

The new light-rail system in use in Salt Lake County is a hybrid between an interurban line from outlying areas and a streetcar line in the capital city. Using modern technology with an expanded bus feeder service bringing business commuters and shoppers to the stations, only one or two light-rail lines are necessary to handle the mass transit needs of the county for years to come.

With the tracks gone from behind the station, the building is now the home of the Utah State Historical Society.

QUIET VILLAGE
Watercolor 18" x 25" 1998

There are two ways to render a station. One is train time. Baggage handlers, sacks of mail, steam from the cars, and hustle and bustle of people coming and going. All make for an exciting painting. I have painted such scenes many times. The other way is to do just the opposite. No trains, no people, just empty tracks. I decided to do the latter for this one. I wanted to make it during the winter, short days and snow. The Western Pacific and the Denver & Rio Grande Western scheduled most trains to arrive and depart in the morning and evening hours. I decided to do the station at a little after 4:00 p.m. A Salt Lake Transit trolley and a carriage or two would make the scene alive but quiet.

This painting takes me back to the many stations I have visited. Some have been very crowded with people running to catch trains, others silent. Some did not have trains at all. When the train came into the station it filled all the senses. The smell of the hot steam that used to permeate the platforms mixed with the aromas from the diner. Today, the smell of steam is gone as electric heating and air conditioning have replaced the steam-operated type. And the aroma from the diner has changed, but train time is still exciting. Still there is something about the silence before or after train time. The ticket agents are going over travel routes or taking phone calls. A janitor sweeps the floor and empties ash trays. A waitress and cook chat at the counter in the coffee shop, and one or two men read the paper as they wait for a train. A child's laughter echoes through the empty waiting room and the staccato clicks of typewriters from the offices up around the waiting area all add to the sounds of the waiting passenger. Out on the platform a locomotive crew waits by their steed to add cars to the incoming train as express agents double-check paperwork and packages. All this happened day after day between train times in stations all across this land.

Quiet Village is just one of those times that is between trains and between the snows of another storm.

Chapter 6

Sage and Snow, Steam and Steel

Western Pacific Railroad near Low, Utah
1938

O ften referred to as "the railroad that was built too late," the Western Pacific Railway was constructed from Salt Lake City to Oakland, California, between 1903 and 1909. By the end of the 19th century, several transcontinental rail systems had been built. The Northern Pacific, the Great Northern and the Milwaukee Road railroads competed along the northern routes, just south of the Canadian border. The Southern Pacific and the Santa Fe railroads did the same along the southern areas. But only the Union Pacific/ Central Pacific system extended west beyond Salt Lake City.

Several Midwestern railroads reached Denver, Colorado Springs and Pueblo, Colorado, notably the Missouri Pacific, Burlington Route, Rock Island, and Kansas Pacific. The Kansas Pacific was aligned with the Union Pacific, but the others were competitors and turned most of their westward business over to the Rio Grande Western, which terminated at Ogden, Utah. Although on friendly terms with the Central Pacific in Ogden, the Rio Grande Western was not given preference over the Union Pacific's heavy tonnage at Ogden, so sometimes shipments languished till a train could be made up.

George Gould, son of famous rail baron Jay Gould, was highly involved with the Missouri Pacific and Rio Grande and felt that a connection should be made to the West Coast that would more effectively compete with Union Pacific/Central Pacific. By 1899, the Central Pacific had been absorbed into the Southern Pacific and was under control of the Union Pacific. So, in 1901 George Gould then turned to the anticipated Los Angeles & Salt Lake, presided over by Senator John Clark, to see if a deal could be worked out to southern California. Unfortunately, Clark had secretly agreed with Union Pacific's president, E.H. Harriman, to join forces to build the vital link between those two cities and Gould was left out.

The only recourse was to build his own road directly west from Salt Lake City to the San Francisco Bay area. Although he succeeded in obtaining much of the necessary funding from various banks, in essence, he also raided the treasury of the Rio Grande and Missouri Pacific railroads to help. This resulted in the bankruptcy of the Rio Grande, and he was forced to step down as vice-president.

Two other interesting sidelights demanded by the bankers were that, 1- the new railroad would be strictly a bridge route, running traffic only between Oakland and Salt Lake City with no side branches which would dilute the funds needed for the overland construction. 2- The railroad would be surveyed and built so that the maximum grade on the entire line would be only 1 percent.

Although other routes were considered, the only one that fit the 1 percent gradient ran up the Feather River from Sacramento, California, over the Sierra Nevada Range through a 6000-foot tunnel just under the lowest pass at Chilcoot, then through Nevada's Great Basin. Even then, the route shared the Humboldt River valley, between Winnemucca and Wells, with the Southern Pacific for 177 miles. A few miles west of the Utah/Nevada boundary, the rail builders were required to construct a 270 degree horseshoe curve and cut through part of the mountain at Silver Zone.

Most of the grading between Salt Lake City and the Nevada border was simple. Aside from a few miles through the gap between the Cedar and Lakeside mountain ranges, between Clive and Delle, the rest of the line was just raised up above the absolutely level salt flats or at the southern edge of the Great Salt Lake. A 32-mile stretch beginning just east of Wendover has the distinction of being the longest and most level piece of railroad in the United States.

Because it is a bridge route for through traffic only, despite being connected with the Rio Grande, tonnage was still light requiring a bond issue to provide funds to upgrade the line. As a result, in 1915 the railway went into receivership, coming back out as the reorganized Western Pacific Railroad in 1916. At this time, the railroad was allowed to build or to buy side branches that finally helped it to become barely profitable. It existed in this state until 1981 when the entire route was merged into the Union Pacific as its Feather River Division. The line was upgraded to Union Pacific's high construction and maintenance standards. It became a highly efficient route and has competed with Southern Pacific's overland route, despite being 170 miles longer between Utah and the Bay Area. Ironically, the Western Pacific's original nemesis then became its owner, and the Southern Pacific then had to develop a better working relationship with the Rio Grande. Subsequently, in the late 1980's, the Southern Pacific and the Rio Grande merged their lines together.

Despite a maximum one percent grade, compared to Southern Pacific's more than 2.5 percent grades, even the lower percentage is still fairly stiff when there are a hundred or more loaded cars behind a locomotive. As tonnage increased on Western Pacific's overland route, helper engines were needed on the steepest sections, until huge articulated engines with 12 and 16 driving wheels were purchased. Between 1917 and 1938, 20 articulated-types of 2-6-6-2 and 2-8-8-2 wheel arrangements were delivered from the American and Baldwin locomotive companies. Steam engines were designated according to their wheel arrangements—the first number being the number of leading or pilot wheels, the last being the number of wheels under the firebox and cab, and the number(s) between being the number of driving wheels. A single number for conventional engines and two number for articulated locomotives.

Then in late 1938, seven 4-6-6-4 engines of the Challenger type, originally developed by the Union Pacific, were bought from The American Locomotive Company, Schenectady, New York. Designated as the M-100 class, these engines were 120 feet long, built with large 70-inch driving wheels and weighed 509,000 pounds (295 tons). The tender had a capacity of 25 tons of coal and 22,000 gallons of water. When the Western Pacific was completely dieselized in the early 1950's, its steam fleet was generally sold for scrap or to a few other lines that were still using steam engines.

Although no Western Pacific articulated engines were salvaged, the image of Challenger #403 has been preserved on paper. The painting shows this hulkingly magnificent engine with a long eastbound manifest freight cresting the 0.8 percent grade on a winter afternoon in 1938 just west of Low with the Lakeside Mountains in back.

SAGE AND SNOW, STEAM AND STEEL

Oil 18"x 24" 1997

Big steam! I love it! One of the main reasons I wanted to do this book was to paint some of the large steam locomotives that I hadn't previously painted or that I wanted to paint in a setting of my choosing. For the Western Pacific that meant their large 4-6-6-4 Challenger type.

The Western Pacific was the last of the transcontinental railroads to be built. In actuality it was the western expansion to the Denver & Rio Grande Western. The line from Salt Lake to the bay area of California was complete in 1909. Because of the lateness of the building, the Western Pacific was able to keep its grades to or below one percent (gradient percentage = how much vertical rise there is in a run of 100 feet, hence a one percent grade would equal a rise of one foot per every hundred feet of horizontal run. A two percent grade would equal a rise of two feet per 100 feet of horizontal run, etc.)

While the Western Pacific didn't have the volume of traffic the Southern Pacific had, it was still a busy well-maintained railroad. As the United States came out of the Great Depression, traffic picked up for all the railroads. Europe was in war and goods were being sent to help our Allies. For the eastern portion of the Western Pacific, the railroad employed large 2-8-2 Mikado locomotives. While these were the state of the art, the Western Pacific wanted something with a little more get-up-and-go to it. In 1936 the Union Pacific along with American Locomotive Works (ALCO) came up with a new 4-6-6-4 wheel arrangement. The Western Pacific was so impressed with what Union Pacific's new 4-6-6-4s could do, that in 1938, they ordered seven larger locomotives to run between Salt Lake City, Utah, and Elko, Nevada.

The new locomotives were exactly what the railroad needed. Soon mile long freight trains were running across the salt flats at 70 mph. The locomotives weighed 1,009,000 pounds, had 70 inch drivers, 265 psi of steam pressure and developed 100,000 pounds of tractive effort. These were large and fast locomotives.

In choosing where to paint the locomotive, I had thoughts of putting it in Weber or Echo Canyons. True, that is Union Pacific territory, however after the Western Pacific retired the locomotives in 1950, the Union Pacific used them out of Ogden for helpers up to Wahsatch, Utah. What a great painting that would have made. A Union Pacific 4-8-8-4 with a Western Pacific 4-6-6-4 on the point! Someday I will have to do one just for fun. For this painting however, I chose to keep the 4-6-6-4 on home rails. Challenger 403 has just crested the top of the grade at Low, Utah, and is skirting the Cedar Mountains. I like these locomotives! I wish this was still hanging in my studio. These were great locomotives and aesthetically one of the most pleasing locomotives I have ever painted.

Chapter 7

Big Steam at Covered Bridge

Denver & Rio Grande Western in Spanish Fork Canyon
1943

In 1890, the Denver & Rio Grande Railway in Colorado, along with its associate, the D&RGW Railway in Utah, known as the "Baby Railroad" due to its three-foot narrow gauge existence, was standard-gauged as the Rio Grande Western, then subsequently reorganized as the Denver & Rio Grande Western Railroad. Since then, the D&RGW has been one of the most observed and photographed of American railroads. Due to its numerous tunnels, much curvature, steep grades over Tennessee Pass in Colorado and Soldier Summit in Utah, and delightful scenery in the mountainous areas, the railroad has drawn more than its share of interest. This despite its relative remoteness from large population centers and rather short operation—just 570 miles via the Moffat Tunnel (745 miles via the Royal Gorge).

Besides its numerous branches built into the silver mining areas in the Colorado Rockies, it was also originally conceived as a possible transcontinental route to compete with the Union Pacific just to the north and other iron roads to the south. However, it mainly evolved into a bridge route handling traffic between the Burlington Route, the Rock Island Line, and the Missouri Pacific on the east and the Western Pacific on the west. Added to this were several important on-line industries, notably the coal mines in both Utah and Colorado. When it purchased the Denver & Salt Lake Railroad, which had built west from Denver and ran out of funds at Craig, Colorado, this road became a major branch with even more coal producing facilities.

Several branch lines were developed in Utah, as well, mainly to coal mines in eastern Utah, and to silver mines in Park City, the Tintic area and clear down to Marysvale in the deep south-central part of the state.

For most of the steam years, until the early 1950's, typical freight trains would be pulled by whatever power the yardmasters and dispatchers could round up. The standard freight locomotives such as Mikados and Consolidations were common, but ponderous articulated engines were often needed to haul the tonnage over the various mountain ranges. Many books have been written and photos taken of these mighty engines and their servicing facilities in the mountains of Colorado, although not as much as been so considered in the mountains and canyons of Utah. Most books were written by Easterners, and once they did their work in Colorado, they returned to the East to have them published and generally didn't venture another 500 miles farther west to Utah.

In the diesel era, since the early 1950's, as competition became more intense, the D&RGW, had a shorter route than Union Pacific between Salt Lake City and major industrial centers in the central mid-west, such as Kansas City and St. Louis, Missouri. Nonetheless it was still considered as having less capability than the big railroad. For decades, since then, to demonstrate to shippers and large customer industries that it could compete and offer good service, on-time performance, and such, the Rio Grande operated many more shorter, faster trains than the typically long trains run by its competitors. Not only were these shorter trains easier to dispatch, rather than having to wait for many dozens of cars to accumulate and be made up into a train, they were much easier to handle up and down the steep mountains for which the Grande was noted.

Passenger service was not neglected on the D&RGW, either. Early on there were passenger accommodations on most branches and on such long distance trains as the *Scenic Limited*, the *Exposition Flyer,* and later the *Prospector* between Utah and Colorado.

As mentioned, the Rio Grande route was also noted for much impressive scenery. In the early 1950's, the Rio Grande, in cooperation with the Burlington Route and the Western Pacific, developed what many have said was the nation's most attractive train running through the most beautiful scenery—the *California Zephyr.* Starting westward from Chicago, the solid stainless-steel train, including several vista dome coaches, was pulled by Burlington's silver diesels to Denver. The D&RGW then put on its impressive gold, black, and silver engines for the run to Salt Lake. The Western Pacific's handsome orange and silver units then took the train the remaining distance to Oakland, California.

The schedule was designed so that the most interesting scenery would be observable during the daylight hours. The westbound train left Chicago at 3:10 p.m., arriving in Denver at 8:20 the next morning. Both the Colorado Rockies and Utah's Wasatch Mountains were crossed before nightfall; then the Feather River canyon in California's Sierra Nevadas was traversed the next morning. The train arrived at Oakland at 3:10 p.m., 48 hours after leaving Chicago. The reverse route had the train leaving Salt Lake City at 5:45 a.m. in order to catch both the Wasatch and Rocky mountain ranges in daylight. Although the *Zephyr* was not an all-Pullman train, it was an extra-fare operation so that the clientele was above average in means and appearance. Each of the stainless-steel cars was prefixed by the word Silver, then a type of tree, animal or astronomical object, such as *Silver Aspen, Silver Antelope* and *Silver Planet.*

As the inexorable crunch began to be felt by all passenger railroads, with people taking to automobiles or airplanes in favor of trains, the *California Zephyr* eventually had to be discontinued. Finally the train stopped running in 1970, much to the dismay of passengers, train crews and the general public. The D&RGW then continued to run a shortened version between Salt Lake and Denver renamed the *Rio Grande Zephyr* up into the 1980's before it was allowed to be shut down. And, although Amtrak's *California Zephyr* runs along the same route through Utah, it isn't quite the same, mainly because Amtrak's equipment looks the same no matter where one observes it around the country.

Gil has painted a view of bygone days—a massive D&RGW 2-8-8-2 articulated class L-131 locomotive thunders eastward through Spanish Fork canyon in 1943, some three miles west of Thistle, passing the tiny community of Covered Bridge. Not only has steam been gone for almost half a century, the covered bridge has also been removed. Only memories remain.

BIG STEAM AT COVERED BRIDGE

Oil 18" x 24" 1998

The Denver & Rio Grande Western's main line over Soldier Summit has always been one of my favorite places to chase, photograph and paint trains. The line from Provo to Helper is very scenic and it is entertaining to watch trains as they battle the steep grades. Helpers (extra locomotives put in the middle or on the end of a train) are the norm, not the exception.

I had always wanted to paint one of D&RGW's big articulated locomotives running past the covered bridge area. Bob agreed but added, "Make it during the World War II era." As I thought about it, this made sense. It would have been impossible to win the war without the railroads or the steam locomotive.

As the war in Europe progressed, the railroads found themselves playing catch-up as the amount of traffic on all railroads increased almost weekly. Many railroads ordered new locomotives and rebuilt others that had been put in storage during the Great Depression. From 1941 to 1945 the railroads moved 90 percent of all passenger, freight and wartime materials. The amount in billions of tons moved for one year wasn't to be equaled until 1996. Without the railroads of the United States the two-front war we were fighting would have been lost or extended many years past the 1945 date of V-J Day.

As my tribute to the men and women that moved the freight, passengers and materiel of war, I decided to paint #3607 at Covered Bridge. The trains consist contains munitions, three cars holding six Sherman tanks, and a string of tank cars from the oil fields of California. More cars extend down the canyon, and this train will undoubtably have a helper added at Thistle to boost it over the 7,440-foot summit.

Why I chose #3607 is two-fold. One is that when built, these mammoth locomotives were the "world's largest." Built in 1927 they were also the most powerful locomotives on earth at the time. The locomotive weighed 649,000 pounds It had 63 inch drivers, 240 psi of steam pressure, four 26 inch x 32 inch cylinders and 132,000 pounds of tractive effort. Along with the tender, these locomotives weighed in at 992,000 pounds. These locomotives were so successful that the Western Pacific, Duluth Missabe & Iron Range, and others copied the boiler for their large 2-8-8-2 and 2-8-8-4 locomotives. Because of the successful design the D&RGW ordered 10 more heavier copies (classed L-132) in 1930. They lasted until 1956 pushing and pulling trains all over the D&RGW system.

The other reason I chose this locomotive is that it is photographer Dick Kindig's favorite. Dick photographed many different railroads and he took the photo after which I based this painting. I hope you like it, Mr. Kindig.

Chapter 8

Morning Pastoral

Utah Idaho Central in the Cache Valley
1946

Power and poles from Payson to Preston. As electric power began to catch on across the nation around the beginning of the 20th century, various companies had developed the ability to generate high voltages and to transmit the electrical power for long distances. This made it possible to run light-weight trains on standard-gauged tracks using electricity to power the train. Although the initial cost of constructing electric motors and building them onto passenger trains along with the erection of hundreds of miles of supporting poles, wires and generating plants was quite substantial, the subsequent maintenance of an electrical system was much less costly than for a comparable steam railroad.

Interurban electric train routes of approximately 50-100 miles sprang up between major metropolitan areas generally within a specific state. Even as early as 1900, many of the steam railroads had discovered that the long-haul movement of goods and passengers was more lucrative than trains that would have to stop every few miles to pick up people or commodities. So electrical power could operate interurban railways, even parallel to major steam roads without incurring the steam railways' objections.

Utah's Wasatch Front (although it was not called that in the first half of the 20th century) was admirably suited to such a venture. With the bulk of the state's population residing between Provo, Spanish Fork and Payson on the south and Ogden, Brigham City and Logan on the north, it was natural that interurban railroads would be considered. The Union Pacific had found it a nuisance to stop at every station between Salt Lake City and Logan, and the Rio Grande found it just as onerous to stop at every town between Salt Lake and Provo. Accordingly, not one but three interurban roads were constructed, each end to end, producing an electrical rail system stretching some 200 miles from north to south.

Originally a steam rail line begun in 1890 by Simon Bamberger, later to be one of Utah's governors, the Great Salt Lake & Hot Springs Railway built northward from Salt Lake City paralleling the Union Pacific. Several years later the name was changed to the Salt Lake & Ogden and in 1917 to the Bamberger Railroad. This railroad was electrified in 1910 operating with 750 volts d.c., the highest voltage of any electric line in the country.

Also in 1890, a small resort railroad was built from Ogden to another Hot Springs resort a few miles north. About 10 years later, this line was taken over by the Ogden Rapid Transit, one of David Eccles' holdings, as the Transit line was expanding in all directions in Ogden. By 1913, the Logan Rapid Transit (another of Eccles' interests) was also expanding northward and southward; then a scant year later when it appeared that interurban railroads were the wave of the future, the Logan Rapid Transit and the Ogden Rapid Transit companies were directed to come together and were merged into the Ogden, Logan & Idaho Railway.

The third of the triumvirate was the Salt Lake & Utah Railroad, begun in 1913 by W.C. Orem. By 1916, this road had reached Provo, had incorporated the Provo trolley system and had been extended on south to Payson where the major shop facilities were located.

Although mainly designed for transporting passengers between the larger cities, as well as smaller towns up and down the lines, much in the way of less-than-carload freight and express items were carried. In addition, all three electric lines owned rather heavy-duty freight engines for use in hauling regular freight cars with a variety of general merchandise, coal, oil, grain and sugar beets. In fact, the Bamberger Railroad was the only line which served the massive Hill Air Force Base and the Army's Ogden Arsenal facility in Clearfield. During the world wars, the Bamberger would often supply entire troop trains in delivering soldiers to and from the major steam road stations and northern Utah military depots.

The builders of the Ogden, Logan & Idaho Railway, in attempting to combine the rapid transit systems of Ogden and Logan, had a problem. The northern station of the Ogden Rapid Transit lay at Brigham City while the southernmost parts of the Logan Rapid Transit were at Hyrum and Wellsville, with the steep Wellsville Mountains in between. The southern pass between Box Elder County and down Sardine Canyon to Cache County was also much too steep for railroad construction. The solution was to utilize the abandoned Utah Northern narrow gauge grade from Deweyville, up over Collinston Hill to Mendon. This two percent grade had been superseded by the flatter route through Bear River Canyon when Union Pacific standard-gauged the former Utah Northern line in 1890. Although some 44 miles of very sparsely-populated area lay between, the new line did provide access to several small villages and ranches. Then, in 1915, the Smithfield branch of the railroad was extended northward to Richmond, Lewiston and across the Idaho line to Franklin, Whitney, and terminating at Preston. The Utah Idaho Central Railroad was organized when the Cache Valley Railroad, a sugar beet hauling road, was merged in 1918.

Interurban railways were even more susceptible to other modes of transportation than were steam passenger roads. Not only did these electric lines parallel many steam lines, they also paralleled practically all the highways between cities. After World War II when automobiles came into general use by American families, there was not much use for mass transit. Bus companies also evolved or services were expanded by Greyhound and Trailways. By the middle 1940's it became apparent that the interurban rail systems, not only in Utah, but throughout most of America, were not to last much longer.

The Salt Lake & Utah was the first to shut down, in March 1946. The Utah Idaho Central followed suit on February 15, 1947. The Bamberger Railroad lasted until September 1952. Not much is left of Utah's electric interurban heritage. The most enduring items being the solidly-built brick depots of the Utah Idaho Central still in use as residences or businesses in many towns from Brigham City to Lewiston.

The painting has Utah Idaho Central car #513 leading train #203 running northward through the Cache County farmlands between Hyrum and Logan in 1946, toward the end of interurban operations.

MORNING PASTORAL

Watercolor 18" x 24" 1998

As I write this in my studio, the equinox has long passed but the snow still falls. When I was asked to do one of Utah's many interurban railroads, I had planned to do one of the Bamberger Line that ran between Ogden and Salt Lake City. The Bamberger Line was my father's favorite to ride. As I was growing up he would tell me stories from his youth. My favorites always had to do with his working at the Lagoon Amusement Park and the Bamberger rides to the park. During his youth the interurban lines would haul train-loads of high school kids to Lagoon for their school's "Lagoon Day". My father would tell me about all the kids hanging out the windows and the various things that would happen on the way. I painted one of these trains for my dad. The train was just out of the station and was headed west to the north-bound tracks at 4th West. I had kids hanging out from every window waving at passers by as well as each other. Every time I see that painting it makes me want to go back to that time to ride these wonderful trains.

The electrified interurban lines stretched from Payson, Utah, on the south all the way up to Preston, Idaho, on the north. One could board one of these trains, divided into three separate lines, and ride to any town between Payson and Preston.

Out of all the interurban line paint schemes, the starburst of the Utah Idaho Central was the most intriguing. I also have always thought that Cache Valley with its several small farming communities, is one of the most picturesque in the state. With that in mind I started this painting. This is one of those paintings that would have worked at any time of day, during any season. I had thought of doing winter first with a stark white snow and deep blue sky. I then thought to make it in fall with the yellows and reds of the trees to back up the green and silver of the cars. I ended up doing spring. The line is at the south end of the valley with some snow still in the surrounding mountains. In keeping with the theme of the Cache Valley, I put in a pasture as well as a marsh. The train is #203 the second morning train from Ogden due to arrive in Logan at 9:32 a.m.

I like this painting. It reminds me of spring. Still, as I type this, the snow falls on this April morning. Soon however, the valleys of Utah will look like this painting once more.

Chapter 9

The Storm Chasers

Union Pacific near Wanship, Utah
1952

Although silver is not magnetic, the way it attracted steel rails would make one think that it was. The silver mines in Park City are a case in point. Before discussing silver, however, it is necessary to go back to the coal mines.

From 1871 to 1876, the 3-foot narrow gauge Summit County Railroad was hauling coal from the mines around Coalville to Echo on the Union Pacific mainline. Union Pacific was being cavalier toward the coal mines in Summit County, however, as they were competing with coal mines on its own properties in southwestern Wyoming. Sometimes coal from the Utah mines was given good rates to transport to Salt Lake Valley, but oftentimes not. Salt Lake consumers were naturally very unhappy at being held hostage by the Union Pacific and wished to get their coal at better rates.

So, in 1880, another narrow gauge line, the Utah Eastern Railroad, began construction from Coalville to Salt Lake City, anticipating coming down Parley's Canyon after a detour to the burgeoning town of Park City with its many valuable silver mines. Always one for a good scrap, Union Pacific, which had bought up

the Summit County Railroad, standard-gauged it in 1880 and began extending it toward Park City, paralleling the Utah Eastern the whole way. Both railroads entered Park City on the same day — December 12, 1880. The two coal railroads began supplying the numerous mines and mills with the necessary coal. The Utah Eastern even had about 40 tons per day extra from the mines on its line and sold this surplus to Salt Lake dealers, unloading the mineral to be hauled over Parley's Summit and down the canyon to the Valley. By 1881, this narrow gauge line was selling enough coal to pay its own way and its bond indebtedness but could not pay to continue its originally planned extension to the Salt Lake Valley, still another 25 miles away over a summit pass and down a steep canyon. Union Pacific's Summit County Railroad, now incorporated as the Echo & Park City Railway once it was standard-gauged, was providing too much competition for the coal business. Besides, there were serious rumors about the D&RGW Railway building into the Salt Lake Valley and bringing Carbon County coal with it.

In 1883, adding further injury, the Union Pacific found a way to buy more of the necessary Utah Eastern bonds and suddenly controlled this railroad as well. Utah Eastern stockholders' litigation failed by 1887, allowing the Union Pacific to do what it wanted, which was to liquidate the Utah Eastern, pull up the rails and ties and use them on other parts of its growing empire, both standard- and narrow-gauged.

Besides hauling all the coal that the mining operations required, the U.P. also brought out much of the ore to be sent to Salt Lake Valley for processing. Ores from Park City, as well as from mines in Alta, the Tintic District and elsewhere around the west and even from Australia, provided much work in the Salt Lake Valley. The various smoke stacks and slag heaps in the neighborhood of the Jordan River are remnants of this thriving, albeit, smoky and sooty industry.

Besides the two railroads mentioned being attracted to Park City, a third was the Salt Lake & Eastern Railway, an outgrowth of John W. Young's railroading enterprises. This line was constructed from Salt Lake City to Park City, using Parley's Canyon that the Utah Eastern had hoped to utilize. Built from 1889 - 1890, the narrow gauge trains on this line brought up much needed merchandise and foodstuffs from the Salt Lake Valley and returned with silver ore to be smelted and refined.

In 1900 the Echo & Park City was officially merged into the Union Pacific and was operated as the Park City branch. A side branch was constructed over to the Keetley mines directly east through the mountain from Park City in 1923, then in 1929, the track along the Weber River bottoms was rerouted to allow construction of Echo Reservoir.

As Park City's mines, and those at Keetley, began to shut down in the 1960's and '70's and other industries in the city were relying on truck transportation, there was essentially no further need for the railroad. Finally, when the chemical plant at Phoston, on the Keetley secondary branch, shut down its operations, there was no recourse but to tear up the rails and leave town. Although there was some discussion about the possibility of connecting this rail line with the Heber Creeper tourist railway in Heber Valley, and operating all the way from Echo to Heber City, the millions of dollars needed for such an operation were nowhere to be found. Practically the entire roadbed from Echo to Park City has been developed into a bicycle and hiking trail, appropriately called the "Rail Trail," managed by the Utah Department of Parks and Recreation.

The element keeping Park City alive and thriving now was a distinct nuisance and hazard back in the mining days: snow. With elevations up to 7000 feet above sea level, winter comes early and hard to the area. All the railroads mentioned utilized a good portion of their revenue keeping their lines open during the winter. Snowplows of various types were needed in attempts to open the track and keep it clear to allow movements of coal and silver ore. A common type of plow was a large wedge-shaped affair pushed by one or several locomotives to move the snow off the rails. However, at times when the snow was too deep or too heavy, any number of engines were insufficient to buck the wedge plows along. At those times, the railroads had to bring in their super power, the large rotary plows. These machines, operated by steam locomotion, were the forerunners of today's home and farm snowblowers. Huge vanes could cut through snow drifts that would only bog down a wedge plow. The cut up snow would then be thrown a hundred or more feet away from the track, clearing the line in good time. These rotaries were expensive to operate and were only used when really necessary.

The rotary plow depicted in this chapter was being used along the Park City branch in about 1951, after having been brought down from Pocatello, Idaho, to Echo. The location is approximately where the westbound lanes of Interstate Highway 80 presently cross above the former rail grade, now the Rail Trail. This very interesting piece of machinery can be seen at the Utah State Railroad Museum.

THE STORM CHASERS
Oil 18"x 24" 1998

One of the most exciting things to see operate on any railroad is the rotary snowplow. When the snow gets too deep for regular plows and Jordan spreaders, the big rotary plows are called out. Almost yearly the snows over Donner Pass will be great enough to pull out the ex-Southern Pacific rotaries to keep the lines clear. The big Union Pacific rotary also usually gets a yearly work-out as snowbound railroads need to clear their lines. Also, without precedence, the ex-Denver& Rio Grande Western's rotary gets its chance to open the Cumbres & Toltec Scenic Railroad in southern Colorado.

One of the most unusual pieces of equipment the Utah State Railroad Museum has acquired is rotary plow 061. Built by ALCO in 1912, this particular rotary snow plow was built for the Oregon, Washington Railroad & Navigation Company. This was Union Pacific's extension into the Northwestern United States. The 061 was stationed mainly in Pocatello, and when needed was moved to other parts of the Union Pacific system.

In 1951 the rotary was modified with a raised pilot's cab. The pilot is the person who controls the speed of the blade as well as gives the directions to the engineers of the rotary and the locomotive(s) pushing behind. Rotary 061 also received a new tender from a 2-10-2, and its original tender was converted into a water car to trail the tender. There are four men aboard the rotary: The pilot who directs the operation, and with him in the pilot house is the track foreman. Alongside of the boiler is the engineer of the rotary. Bell signals from the pilot tell the engineer how fast to run the blade or to reverse the blade of the rotary. Behind them all, on the back of the rotary, is the fireman. He keeps the fuel and water in the boiler so that the rotary will work.

I put the 061 clearing the line to Park City. The "plow train" is just past the area where I-80 heads to Wanship. The locomotive is #2726, one of the regular 2-8-2s that worked the Park City Local in the 1950's.

It is difficult to depict the entire rotary if one wants to picture it throwing snow. Unseen are the flangers and trucks under the unit as well as some steam lines and the frame.

This was a fun painting to do. I love the snow. And putting a hard-working rotary and 2-8-2 with the plow train slowly crossing an open valley was pure pleasure.

UNION PACIFIC 2726

UNION PACIFIC
061
OW R&N

Chapter 10

Moon Glow at Sunset

Union Pacific at Lake Point, Utah
1949

Although freight traffic on any mainline railroad earns the money and pays the wages, passenger operations seem to be the more glamorous and exciting. This was partly due to the faster speeds that passenger trains generally ran back in the days when railroads operated a dozen or more of them, and long freights were simply not designed to travel fast. General merchandise, coal, ore, and grain trains generally all proceeded at about the same speed and all were required to take a side track when a passenger train was due, even a lowly local job.

All throughout the "Golden Age" of passenger rail travel, roughly the decades between 1920 and 1960, long distance travel was almost always accomplished by trains. Air transportation was in its infancy or juvenile period then and a great many people and businesses had not yet developed the trust of airplanes that now is the norm. Bus travel was generally adequate but cramped.

So rail travel was in its prime. Even older coaches had rest room facilities and if a train did not have the luxury of having a dining car, due to a relatively short distance to be traveled, etc., at least there was usually a counter where a snack of some sort was available. And the spaciousness! In the first place, coach and sleeper seats were wide, quite comfortable and roomy; then, at any time, a passenger could get up and walk around, visit another part of the train, admire the scenery from a vista dome or watch the track receding in the distance from the end observation car.

Long before business travelers were required to use the airways to get from office to client in different parts of the country, for example, they would book a passenger car with a compartment or bedroom in which they could study and get ready for the next day's presentations in the city of destination. Then, after several hours' of reading, study and preparation, he would have the porter turn down the bed and the businessman (it was usually a man; nowadays it might just as easily be a woman) would turn in for a decent night's sleep and be rested for work on the morrow.

And celebrity travel. Movie and stage show personalities preferred train travel. It helped them unwind from the demands of their professions, plus they enjoyed the camaraderie of their agents and press people in the lounge cars of the prestigious trains; and there were always dozens of admiring fans aboard the trains.

Up until the 1950's, practically every railroad that owned a mainline of at least 20 miles ran a passenger train. Freight-only roads were almost unheard of, except for a few terminal switching lines. After that decade, as the onerous burdens of subsidizing passenger operations from freight hauling became unduly large, the Interstate Commerce Commission began allowing some smaller roads to do away with passenger trains. Even then, the large railways such as Union Pacific, Santa Fe, New York Central and Pennsylvania complained about the millions of dollars worth of losses they were experiencing every year just to keep running passenger trains. And there were no government price supports, either, such as were found in other industries. Railroads had to earn enough from their freight operations to pay for their losing passenger business.

Finally, in 1971, the federal government stepped in and allowed any railroad to discontinue its passenger business as long as the new government-sponsored passenger organization, originally called Railpax (then shortly after and still known as Amtrak), could use their rails in the new passenger train network. Most railroads jumped at the chance to get rid of passenger trains and only a small handful continued to operate their own. In Utah, the Union Pacific and Southern Pacific opted out of the passenger business; their freight activity was already as much as they could handle at the time. Western Pacific had gone freight-only a year before. The Denver & Rio Grande Western was one of the few roads that continued to stay in the passenger business. Although it continued to lose money, it was preferable than to have to adjust its schedule for whatever Amtrak may have wanted to run on its lines; besides, its name train, the Rio Grande remnant of the fabled *California Zephyr,* now truncated to the *Rio Grande Zephyr,* was still a popular mode of transportation between Salt Lake City and Denver, Colorado.

Union Pacific had a long and storied history running such notable passenger trains as the *Challenger,* the *City of Los Angeles* and the *Portland Rose,* among many others. U.P. helped pioneer the concept of the fast, clean, sleek diesel-powered streamliner. Many of these were extra-fare trains, meaning that in order to ride, a passenger had to be willing to pay an extra amount so as to get to his destination faster than a slower trains Some trains, such as the *City of Los Angeles* were so prestigious that they were all-Pullman trains—only people who could afford the extra sleeping space could take these trains.

As part of the development of the streamliner concept, General Motors along with the Pullman Standard Company produced an early version of the streamlined train called the *Train of Tomorrow.* It toured the country in 1947 showing what the railroads were doing to make travel more comfortable and exciting. One of the most unusual aspects at the time was the construction of the vista dome on the cars. This feature allowed passengers to ride above the general roof line of the train, enclosed by glass windows so that they could enjoy the expansive scenery unfolding with every curve, especially in the West.

After this train finished its tour, it was purchased intact by Union Pacific and used almost exclusively between Portland and Seattle as train 457/458, the *Domeliner.* Upon retirement of the train in 1963, many of the cars, including the dome observation/lounge car named the *Moon Glow,* were sold to a used equipment dealer in Pocatello, Idaho. The Promontory Chapter of the National Railway Historical Society obtained the *Moon Glow* from the dealer and later presented it to the Utah State Railroad Museum. The car is presently undergoing restoration to its prime (1950's) status.

Although the *Moon Glow* ran through Utah only once on its way to southern California before being sent to the Northwest, Gil's artistic license shows the car as if it had run on the end of the westbound *"City of Los Angeles"* at Lakepoint with Western Pacific mainline and the Great Salt Lake in back.

MOON GLOW AT SUNSET

Watercolor 18"x 24" 1998

Train travel. There is nothing like it. One can sit back, relax and take in the sights. I love to take the trains. As Edna St. Vincent Millay wrote: "...yet there isn't a train I wouldn't take, no matter where it is going." I feel the same way.

During my life, I have traveled to many places. I have been to all of the United States except North Dakota, North Carolina and Alaska. I will remedy this soon. I have also been to many countries outside of the United States and have flown, driven, cruised and ridden the trains. The way I prefer to go is by train. Some consider me a little larger than normal. At 6' 1" and 240 pounds I don't seem large until I try to pry myself into an airline seat.

Real travel to me, is rail travel. The Union Pacific had some of the finest trains anywhere. Their *City* trains were, in fact, moving cities. One could board and get a hair cut or style, eat some of the best food in the country from fresh trout to prime rib and then go back and recline in an oversized seat. If you wanted to pay a little extra, you can get a private room, complete with beds, table and your very own bathroom! The *City* trains of yesterday were the epitome of luxury. How I long for their return.

Amtrak is doing just that. Although not quite up to the standards of the old trains, the food, amenities, and seats are wonderful. I have ridden many of Amtrak's trains and have enjoyed the food, the ride and the new people that I have met onboard. When I take Amtrak and arrive at my destination, I am not tired! Imagine that.

For this painting I would rather have done the *City of Los Angeles* from the locomotive end. However, the museum had the back end and wanted a painting of the *Moon Glow* observation car. The *City of Los Angeles* departed Salt Lake City at 4:40 p.m. during the 1950's. I wanted it to be cold outside, while those inside the train would be warm, some starting the first dinner selections as the landscape rolled by. A winter sky with the train westbound close to the Great Salt Lake and a sliver of a moon in the sky, all seemed to fit what I wanted. The many compound curves of the observation car gave me a few problems but they were soon solved and the rest of the painting fell into place. I like the way this turned out, so much so, that I wish I was on this train instead of painting it.

Chapter 11

Titan of the Wasatch

Union Pacific Railroad in Weber Canyon
1950

W hat does one call the largest, heaviest and most powerful steam locomotive on earth? Big Boy! That seemingly casual and irreverent moniker was not originally intended to be the name of the monstrous engine of the 4-8-8-4 wheel arrangement.

Although Union Pacific was known for getting merchandise over the road in good time, for eastbound traffic leaving Ogden, the obstacle known as the Wasatch Mountains often required additional locomotives and crews in order to keep the cars moving. The railroad's 4-6-6-4 Challenger locomotives were essentially doing the required job, but shippers and receiving merchandise companies wanted even faster service. By 1940, it appeared that the nation might be forced into the world war that had already been raging for two years. More traffic was expected and the steep grades of the Wasatch were going to be an impediment. Union Pacific had already developed two large, efficient and fast engines—the FEF (4-8-4) passenger type and the 4-6-6-4 Challenger freight engine. So the company's mechanical department working with the American Locomotive Company designed an even larger engine specifically to pull heavier trains, faster up over the Wasatch range — more tons at more miles per hour.

Because of ALCO's success at building the two previous models, it took only a little over a year's time to design, develop and construct the large 4-8-8-4 locomotive. And the engine exceeded all hopes. Weighing 772,000 pounds (engine alone), along with the tender capacity of 25,000 gallons of water and 28 tons of coal, developing 6000 hp, this brute could haul over 4500 tons (a heavy train at the time) up Weber and Echo canyons faster than any previous engine or sets of engines, then race along the high Wyoming plains at 60-70 mph.

Because this was a new wheel arrangement, a new name was to be given to the class. At railroad headquarters, the new type was to be given the name Wasatch, in honor of where the locomotive was to operate. However, before this was known outside of the corporate hierarchy, as the first engine of this type was being manufactured on the erecting floor in Schenectady, New York, a machinist wrote on the large blank smokebox front, "BIG BOY." Immediately everyone involved with the project started calling it by that. The name took off so fast and completely that the company officials just let their name be filed away almost to be forgotten, and the huge machines have been "Big Boys" ever since.

The first one, #4000, was put to work in 1941, with 24 to follow, the last being built in 1944. And right in time, too. With the United States entering World War II in December 1941, these new engines were admirably suited to handling more heavy trains faster, not only over the Wasatch between Ogden and Green River, Wyoming, but also over Sherman Hill, another relatively stiff obstacle in southern Wyoming, and into Cheyenne. These machines then freed many smaller types for use during the war.

Troop trains by the hundreds transported our armed forces personnel to and from the two coasts, as the nation was fighting battles beyond both our east and west shores.

Many trains that the "Big Boys" pulled were solid war materiel consists for the West Coast, and brought solid trains of perishable fruits and vegetables to the nation's consumers and to military facilities. At times, cars full of refrigerated meats would be added to the trains. Although all rail lines around the country were involved in keeping pace with the war, Union Pacific's overland mainline was one of the busiest providing service to the San Francisco area as well as the Los Angeles/Long Beach harbors. The railroad's dependable "Big Boys" kept things moving as well or better than were intended.

The war ended and the big engines were assigned to standard, regular manifest trains—even an occasional passenger train if it needed to get to a division point on time. The locomotives worked so well that they were the pride of the railroad from the president down to the switchmen and engine wipers. Everyone talked about them and when one of them rumbled by, the nearby track gangs would step back and admire the huge beasts.

On occasion, two of the "Big Boys" would be double-headed (coupled together) to an exceptionally heavy trains. When blasting uphill at 25 mph in Weber Canyon, next to old U.S. Highway 30, the noise would be so deafening that car and bus passengers were known to hold their hands over their ears as the canyon reverberated to the cacophony of sound.

By the end of their lives, as diesel-electric locomotives and turbines were taking over the freight duties, the "Big Boys" were still performing marvelously, putting on over 7000 miles per month each before having the required inspections, servicing and overhauling. By the time they were retired, each of the initial 20 engines, built in 1941 and 1942, had accumulated more than a million miles of travel, with #4006 having run 1,064,625 miles.

These locomotives were superior in many ways to almost all other large, steam motive power, and in some ways even to diesel locomotives. But due to the labor-intensive operation and maintenance common to all steam engines, these magnificent machines were finally retired in the very late 1950's and early 1960's.

Union Pacific had the foresight to save eight of the engines from the scrapper's cutting torches and donated them to various museums around the country, although none of them to Ogden, the western terminus. At that time, Ogden was an active junction city terminal for three railroads, and the museum that the Ogden Union Station is now was not considered. It is unfortunate that there isn't a "Big Boy" in Ogden, but the eight remaining engines can be viewed. They are located in: Pomona, California; Cheyenne, Wyoming; Denver, Colorado; Omaha, Nebraska; St. Louis, Missouri; Dallas, Texas; Green Bay, Wisconsin and Scranton, Pennsylvania.

"Big Boy" #4024 is shown climbing the 1.14 percent grade a little up-canyon from Gateway, just east of the power plant near the mouth of Weber Canyon, with a solid block of refrigerator cars from central California. The Southern Pacific had brought the train loaded with perishable produce such as lettuce, tomatoes, artichokes and many kinds of fruit across the Sierra Nevada Mountains and handed it over to the Union Pacific at Ogden.

TITAN OF THE WASATCH

Oil 18"x 24" 1998

My favorite locomotives to paint are Union Pacific's huge 4-8-8-4 locomotives. The 4024 was the last of the "Big Boys" built for the Union Pacific in 1944. As delivered it weighed in at 1,209,000 pounds and they are commonly known as "world's largest locomotives". The grades of the Wasatch out of Ogden have always been the proving grounds for Union Pacific motive power. The 65-mile 1.14 percent grade up Weber and Echo Canyons have brought difficult operational problems to the railroad. The main traffic flow of the UP goes from west to east and the main barrier has always been the Wasatch Mountains. From the beginning, the Union Pacific would put its newest and largest power in Ogden to battle the Wasatch. If the Wasatch hadn't been such a hinderance, the new wheel arrangements of the 4-6-6-4 and 4-8-8-4 would have never been created.

Ever since the joining of the rails on May 10, 1869, trains off the Central Pacific would be forwarded east out of Ogden. As the lines from the northwest and southwest joined in Ogden, more and heavier trains stomped out of the yards. During the height of the war years, 1943-1944, 70 to 80 trains a day would move up Weber Canyon. The gradient and the need to keep the railroad fluid for troop and passenger trains kept this area a constant headache to dispatchers.

The 4-8-8-4 was built to tackle this problem. The "Big Boy", as they were nicknamed, were built specifically to take a 3,500-ton train up the grade unassisted. As time went on, trains of 4,200 to 4,800 tons were handled by a single "Big Boy". The locomotive could run across the level at 70 mph with whatever it could take up "the hill" from Ogden. The boiler produced 7050 hp with a steady 6000 hp at the drawbar. It had 68 inches drivers, stood 16 feet 2 inches at the stack and had four 24 inch x 32 inch cylinders that produced a tractive effort of 135,000 pounds. The tender held 25,000 gallons of water and 32 tons of coal to be converted to a steam pressure of 300 psi. The locomotive was so large that new 135-foot turntables were added to the Ogden, Green River, and Laramie engine terminals. This locomotive was truly the high-water mark of steam power in the United States.

I have painted many of these 4-8-8-4s, and for this book was going to put one on the LA&SL in southern Utah as they were tested there in 1941 and 1942. I also wanted to put it in Echo but decided instead to put one where no one had ever painted one: in the depths of Weber Canyon. Photos of where I wanted the train located do not exist so I went on a long hike and took the photo myself. I found what I thought was the perfect place. One of the "s" curves deep in the canyon on the 1.14 percent grade with fall colors, snow and the Weber River in the background. I also depicted the locomotive with a clean fire, not much smoke, as that is really how most steam locomotives ran. Do I like the result? Yes! I believe this to be one of the finest renderings of a 4-8-8-4 I have ever painted or seen.

Chapter 12

Whistles in the Night

Ogden Union Station
1951

Ogden: Junction City of the West. For many decades, that is just the way it was. But in the early days of Utah railroading, no one knew that Ogden would be so prominent in Utah and western railroading. Not even when the Central Pacific was allowed to purchase Union Pacific's track from Promontory to Ogden in late 1869 was it apparent. When the Utah Central was built from Ogden to Salt Lake City in 1870, and then as rail lines extended in various directions from the capital city, Ogden was an obvious junction, but still was not particularly important. When the Utah Northern started constructing its narrow-gauged rails to the north, and the city of Corinne began to fade in importance did it appear that Ogden was very strategically placed to capture a lot of traffic in all directions.

In the first few years of the 1900's, Ogden's place was securely set for almost the next century. The Los Angeles & Salt Lake Railroad had been completed from Salt Lake City to the Los Angeles basin. The narrow gauge lines striking northward from Ogden had been standard-gauged and had become an important route to Montana and the northwest. All Union Pacific traffic, freight and passenger, from the east bound for any point in Utah, Nevada or California had to come through Ogden. And, of course, the same held true for all eastbound traffic. All traffic between Omaha, Nebraska, and southern California traveled on Union Pacific rails. Union Pacific and Southern Pacific were end-to-end partners on business between the San Francisco Bay area and the Mid-west. E.H. Harriman, influential president of Union Pacific, attempted to purchase Southern Pacific and bring it into his system, but the federal government forbade that at the time.

As the West Coast became more settled and populated, freight trains and passenger travel accommodations had to keep up with demands for goods and services. This resulted in the double-tracking of most of the Union Pacific mainline between Salt Lake City and Omaha and increasing the number and length of freight and passenger trains.

By the 1940's, at least 10 named passenger trains passed through Ogden each day in each east-west direction. Fabled names such as the *City of San Francisco, City of Los Angeles, Pacific Limited, Los Angeles Limited,* the *Challengers, California Fast Mail* and the *Pony Express* all entered the Ogden Union Station to discharge and pick up passengers and some to have their cars switched around and rearranged. In addition, the *Butte Special* between Salt Lake City and Butte, Montana, ran through Ogden; and several local passenger jobs originated or terminated in Ogden, such as the Malad local and the Cache Valley mixed. Ogden Union Station along with the Ogden Union Railway and Depot Company (a joint switching operation of both U.P. and S.P.) was a busy place all day long, and that was just referring to passenger trains. In addition, a whole parade of freight trains originated, came into or through town, most of which required changes of crews and/or locomotives.

Originally, most passenger trains were dispatched at sufficiently different times through a 24-hour day so that no more than two regular-sized trains would be in the depot at a time, which allowed the train crews time to discuss matters pertaining to the routes and for switch crews to handle any needed shunting. By the 1960's, however, most railroads around the country found that they needed to consolidate schedules to cut down the number of passenger cars, locomotives and manpower and still provide meaningful service to a still-loyal and busy group of passengers.

Union Pacific (and Southern Pacific's Overland Route, of necessity) then arranged their dispatching schedules so that the westbound *City of St. Louis* from St. Louis and the combined *City of Los Angeles/City of San Francisco* from Chicago both arrived in Ogden within a half an hour of each other, comprising up to 55 cars, at around 7:10 p.m. At that time, four switch engines descended on the terminal, two at each end of the trains, and hustled in and out between the two trains and the adjacent drill tracks, shifting cars from one train to another, splitting the two *City* trains from Chicago into two separate trains, adding mail cars from other trains which had accumulated during the day, pulling out cars that were to terminate in Ogden — and accomplished all this in one hour. The same activity occurred with the eastbound trains at about 9:00 each morning. The switching crews at the time took their jobs seriously yet felt it was just part of the daily routine and didn't think there was anything they couldn't do in the given amount of time available. (Incidentally, at this time, a full-course sirloin steak dinner aboard one of America's three all-Pullman trains, the *City of Los Angeles*, went for the wallet-crunching price of $4.75.)

During the 1950's, the time generally depicted in this painting, a lot of general switching work was required at Union Station. Even without the massive switching, there were still cars to be set out, shifted to other trains or rearranged according to what may have been required at the next terminal. This was also the decade of transition. In the early years of the decade, many local passenger and mixed trains were pulled by steam locomotives and most freight was still using steam. However, new diesel-electric locomotives began showing up in increasing numbers, not only for sleek passenger trains but also for freight trains. By the end of the decade, steam was gone entirely. Diesel engines of various builders were constructed in a variety of configurations for freight, passenger and switching requirements. Because of their general improved cleanliness and basically increased horsepower when used together, the diesel locomotive had shown general superiority.

The last steam locomotives used in Ogden were the massive "Big Boys" hauling long freight trains up and down Weber Canyon, and the little 0-6-0 switch engines that for many decades had faithfully done their jobs tirelessly switching the passenger terminal as well as both the Union Pacific and Southern Pacific freight yards. Union Pacific switcher #4436 works the front end of a passenger train at Union Station while a new Southern Pacific ALCO PA-1 diesel quietly idles farther back. This switcher was donated by Union Pacific to the city of Ogden, at one time touching head-to-head with a similar Southern Pacific engine, reminiscent of the Promontory view, in Affleck Park, but is now part of the Utah State Railroad Museum's collection.

WHISTLES IN THE NIGHT
Oil 18" x 24" 1998

On warm summer evenings, I used to lie in bed with my windows open and listen to the whistles in the night. If the air was still or there was a slight breeze from the west, I could hear the engines in the locomotives of the Union Pacific and the Denver & Rio Grande Western accelerate out of town. How I would have longed to hear that in the days of steam. There is nothing more stirring than a train at night and nothing more comforting than the moan of a mournful whistle in the darkness.

The museum ended up with an old Union Pacific 0-6-0. I did my regular research and found that #4436 was one of the regular switch engines assigned to the Ogden Terminal Railroad. The locomotive was built in 1916 by Baldwin Locomotive Works. It has 51 inch drivers, 21 inch x 26 inch cylinders and 34,400 pounds of tractive effort. The tender of the locomotive was modified when converted from a coal burner to an oil burner between 1933 and 1940. It also had a passenger car vestibule added to the back of the tender for use with passenger cars.

Dr. Carr suggested that we do this with a diesel electric locomotive in the background. At first, I wanted to put in an E-6 or and E-7 but as I started to set up the painting I decided to use an ALCO PA. At first this was a Union Pacific PA but to add some color I decide to go with the Southern Pacific PA in the *Daylight* scheme. As I continued to set up the painting, what I had sketched out at the north end of the station quickly changed to the south end. I arranged the switcher so that it would be on track 5 with the PA on track 4. The *Butte Special* is on track 2, and the station platforms, station and express house fill out the right side of the painting. I wanted this to be at night with a full moon and the mountains in the background. However the more I thought about it, a light rain and low clouds would enhance the lights of the city and also add reflections. My brother, his history teacher and I made many journeys to Ogden in the early 1970's and I remember many nights on the platform watching as Amtrak's *San Francisco Zephyr* would glide in, change locomotives and head west. The steam from the cars would engulf the platforms as workers serviced the trains. I had to put this memory in the painting. I also had to put in the different yard workers and inspectors.

The finished painting has the little 0-6-0 adding some head-end cars to train #6, the Eastbound *Mail and Express*. To those that remember the time when these little locomotives worked at all the stations across this nation, I hope this brings back warm memories of the simpler, graceful times of the past.

Chapter 13

Stall for a Thoroughbred

Union Pacific in Ogden
1957

Union Pacific has always been noted for its class act in accommodating the railway passenger. From the initial times of expanding westward, opening up new territories to homesteading or visiting, the railroad was in the vanguard of promoting and advertising its availability for passengers. Even as passenger service on American railroads began its gradual demise, finally to be taken over by the National Railway Passenger Corporation's Amtrak operations, Union Pacific, along with just one or two other railroads, maintained a class of passenger service for which it was known at the peak of named passenger trains. From somewhat lowly trains such as the *Utahn* or the *Pony Express*, as well as numerous local unnamed passenger trains, up through the First Class trains such as the *City of Los Angeles* and the *Portland Rose*, all employees were taught to treat the passenger with dignity and respect. This was even evident when Amtrak took over in 1971 and used former Union Pacific conductors and attendants on the Union Pacific routes that Amtrak utilized.

Many, if not most, of the passenger trains in the latter stages of steam passenger service were pulled by large engines, such as #833. Even later, these locomotives were also often used as helpers assisting the regular diesel engines on particularly steep areas or with exceptionally long, heavy trains.

These locomotives were designed in three classes, beginning in 1937. Union Pacific, ever watchful for the need for additional power, found that the large 4-8-2 Mountain-type locomotives did not have the speed or the horsepower needed to pull heavy trains up the long, sustained grades of the Utah canyons or the high Wyoming plains without additional helpers or more frequent service stops.

Union Pacific officials determined that they needed a locomotive that could pull a 16-car heavyweight train at a normal speed of 60 up to 70 mph. Locomotive builders had long known that big steam engines with six driving wheels could handle speeds of that order, although possibly not with the horsepower that Union Pacific needed, but it was thought that the extended wheelbase of the eight drivers would cause problems on curves as well as the extra wear and tear occasioned by the number and length of the driving rods. The railroad, however, noted that one of its class of freight engines with 12 driving wheels handled mainline curves very well, although at lower speeds, and decided that eight large drivers were worth evaluating.

Accordingly, after many months of testing and deliberations in 1936-37, the railroad decided to re-engineer the 4-8-4 Northern-type designed somewhat earlier by the Northern Pacific Railway, hence the name 'Northern.'

The first of the 800 class, built by the American Locomotive Company, (ALCO), were designated as FEF-1, meaning the 4-8-4 wheel arrangement. (The Union Pacific never referred to this class as the Northern type as most other roads did.) The locomotives weighed 418,800 pounds and had driving wheels 77 inches in diameter. With large driving wheels, these machines not only operated in the 60-70 mph range easily, but because the driving rods were so well designed, that speeds up to 110 mph were recorded. The first set of these locomotives were numbered from 800 through 819 and were attached to tenders carrying 25 tons of coal and 20,000 gallons of water riding on two six-wheel trucks.

Further testing and development over the next several years produced two more subclasses of the 800 class. Engines numbered from 820 through 834 were designed with 80-inch drivers, providing for even more sustained horsepower at higher speeds. They weighed in at 442,000 pounds; their tenders carried 25 tons of coal and 23,500 gallons of water and rode on 14 wheels, the last 10 of which were rigidly attached to the tender frame, and only the front four-wheel truck swiveled. Because this second set was somewhat larger than the first, these FEF-2 engines were called the 'big FEF's' and the earlier ones the 'little FEF's'. A third order, essentially the same as the second with a few more modifications, were called the FEF-3 subclass and numbered 835-844. The last of these, #844, built in 1943, was the last steam engine manufactured for Union Pacific and has the distinction of being the only steam locomotive on a major railroad in the United States never to have been retired. This engine is still owned, maintained and operated by the railroad for special excursions around the Union Pacific's far-flung system.

The roundhouse was the focal point of a steam locomotive's maintenance. Here, dozens of workers were assigned to inspect, lubricate, repair and overhaul the engines according to railroad and federal government requirements at regularly-specified intervals. Boiler inspections are done every 30 days of operation, and minor and major overhauls are performed after a certain number of miles traveled.

Union Pacific FEF-2 #833 was donated by the railroad to Salt Lake City in 1970 where it resided in Pioneer Park until it was transferred to the ownership of the Utah State Railroad Museum and relocated to Ogden in 1999. It has been cosmetically restored and maintained, and adds immeasurably to the museum's attractions, although it will never be put into operating condition.

The painting shows #833 on the huge 135-foot turntable in Ogden. This was one of a very few turntables of this size ever built by the Union Pacific, notably only between Cheyenne, Wyoming, and Ogden, specifically for turning the massive 4-8-8-4 "Big Boy" locomotives. Because steam engines are designed to operate only in the forward position, unlike modern diesel locomotives that can operate in either direction, turning facilities were needed at any point along a railroad line where a steam engine might have to be turned to take a train back to its home terminal. Tables were built according to the largest type of engine expected to be used in a particular division of the railroad.

The hostler, a shop worker trained to operate a locomotive in the service area, is getting ready to drive the big iron horse into a roundhouse stall for servicing. As a well-sired racehorse needs constant vigilance to maintain his strength and abilities, so the mechanical iron horse requires the same sort of attention in order to obtain the maximum effort for which it was constructed.

STALL FOR A THOROUGHBRED

Oil 18"x 24" 1997

The first large, live, steam locomotive I saw was Union Pacific's huge 4-8-4 #8444. It was May 10, 1969, and the big Northern-type locomotive had pulled a special train into Ogden for the festivities. As an eight-year-old boy, I was impressed. Here was a steam locomotive that had never been retired from service. It had 80 inch drivers that towered over my head. At rest it seemed to live, panting, if you will. Later that day I would see this marvelous steed run. And run it did! I had never before seen a train move with such speed. Standing at a crossing in Farmington, #8444 came on in a full gait at some 90 plus mph. This has left a memory that will remain with me forever.

The Union Pacific owned three classes of 4-8-4 or Northern-type steam locomotives, with a total of 45. The first group, known as the small Northerns, had 77 inch drivers and weighed in at 817,200 pounds. They were purchased in 1937 to pull 1,000-ton passenger trains at 100 mph. As the size and speed of passenger trains increased, the UP ordered 15 more 4-8-4s that were larger and faster. This group, numbered from 820 to 834, had 80 inch drivers, 300 psi steam pressure, weighed 889,500 pounds, and developed 63,800 pounds of tractive effort. The large boiler developed 4,870 hp at a speed range of 50 to 80 mph. As built, these were among the best 4-8-4 types in the world.

The third group of 4-8-4s were patterned after the previous class with only minor modifications to the design. The last one, #844 was never retired from the railroad and still runs today. The #844 (ex-8444) is mostly used for service on special trains; however, in 1997 it was used to help a stalled freight train up Archer Hill in Wyoming.

Union Pacific's #833 was one of the second group or FEF-2 class of locomotive. This locomotive was changed from burning coal to burning waste oil in 1946. Over the years this locomotive was one of the best of the 4-8-4s the UP had. It unofficially hit a speed of 130 mph but as that was against the law, no one ever "fessed up". The large 4-8-4 also was a regular on the Union Pacific's *Overland Limited*. This train stayed powered by steam long after all the other main passenger trains on the system became dieselized. The #833 was also tested on the *City of Los Angeles* to see if the steam locomotives could meet the strict schedule of the streamliners. They found while the 4-8-4 could keep up the schedule of four diesel electrics, it would have to run at speeds in the 100 plus mph range to compensate for the extra time it took the steam locomotive to stop and fill with water.

I wanted do the painting of #833 running at a full 100 plus mph gait somewhere in southern Utah. However, as I had done many of these great locomotives at speed, I thought I should do this one at rest. I had first planned to do #833 in the Ogden roundhouse, with the afternoon sun filtering in the doors and windows of the roundhouse. However, trying to find what the inside of the Ogden roundhouse looked like became a nightmare, so I put it outside. The *Overland Limited* arrived in Ogden at 7:40 p.m. where Union Pacific power would be changed for Southern Pacific power. The locomotive would then be brought to the roundhouse and readied for the east-bound run the next day. So, here is #833 at rest. Marker and mars lights on, blue flag out, simmering under a full moon. A thoroughbred at rest.

Chapter 14

Black Widows on the Lake

Southern Pacific Railroad on the Lucin Cutoff
1960

From 1869, the Central Pacific Railroad and subsequently the Southern Pacific, which bought out the C.P. in 1899, until the turn of the century, struggled to handle trains of ever increasing lengths and weights up over the summit of Utah's Promontory Mountains heading both east and west. Originally freight trains had just a dozen or so cars, and locomotives were relatively small. As tonnage increased, more powerful steam engines were developed to keep pace until by 1900, Southern Pacific found it was using an inordinate amount of resources — man, machine and money — to carry the freight. Extra helper engines were often required in that desolate area, which required more engine crews, more coal and water and more maintenance. Maybe the transcontinental builders had made a mistake going from lake level over the mountains and back to lake level. Possibly Brigham Young had the right idea after all, that of building from Ogden south to Salt Lake City, around the southern shore of the Great Salt Lake, then westward all at essentially the same elevation.

At any rate, Southern Pacific's management and civil engineers determined that something had to be done about the problem.

They could not build a new line south of the lake as the Western Pacific was already surveying and preparing to construct there. And they couldn't build any farther north. The only solution was to build directly west of Ogden right across the lake. Earlier surveys had shown that Bear River Bay, the northeastern arm of the lake, between the South Promontory Range and the flats west of Ogden, had an extreme depth of only about 10 to 16 feet. By 1902, the lake level had dropped some 16 feet exposing much of the lake bottom. The railroad then built a causeway fill about 7.3 miles long between the permanent dry shore west of Ogden across the mouth of the bay to the tip of the Promontory peninsula, appropriately called Promontory Point. This is the only place where it is correct to use the term "Promontory Point."

The engineers then attempted to construct a causeway across the main width of the lake west of the Point. Using rock and gravel from quarries on the west side of the lake as well as from the peninsula, the newly developing fill was extended westward 2.5 miles from the Point and 5.1 miles eastward from Lakeside on the western edge. Attempting to dump millions of cubic yards of fill material in the intervening 12 miles across the deepest part of the lake (20 to 35 feet deep) was too time-consuming, expensive and basically impractical. They then resorted to building a wooden trestle. Securing over 38,250 trees up to 120 feet long, from forests in California, Oregon, Louisiana and Texas, 19 pile-drivers, including some built onto barges sitting in the water, were put to work setting the piles deep into the mud and salt at the bottom.

By early 1904, the trestle was completed, including all the decking, extending about 15 feet above the expected highest water level. Each trestle bent consisted of five piles to support the single track above it. Where passing tracks were required, the bents were composed of nine pilings. This undertaking then produced the longest single bridge across a body of water. The line continued almost due westward until it met with the original route at Lucin, just inside the Utah line. By eliminating the tortuous route over Promontory, the new route was called the Lucin Cutoff.

The finished construction had the desired effect, that of cutting out dozens of extra grade-intensive miles over Promontory Summit, speeding up shipments and decreasing locomotive maintenance. The trestle itself required a lot of maintenance, however, and due to the dry climate, the decking caught fire several times from errant locomotive sparks. Between 1920 and 1927 the original deck was replaced; then between 1943 and 1946, the trestle was strengthened by the addition of an additional piling on each side of every bent, requiring the cutting of several thousand more trees. Even then, the railroad required a permanent 20 mph slow order across the bridge, and a very heavy train could cause the trestle to sway slightly from front to back because the lower 70 percent of the bents were not braced.

In 1942, during the height of World War II, the U.S. War Department requested the Southern Pacific to part with the essentially unused original transcontinental trackage from Corinne, up over Promontory Summit and down to Lucin. From 1904, when the Lucin Cutoff was completed, until 1942, only restricted local traffic had been seen over the Summit. So some 123 miles of rail were taken up to be used in various governmental military and support installations around the west, mostly along the piers in the San Francisco Bay area.

By 1953, Southern Pacific analyzed the trestle and found that in order to keep up with ever-increasing tonnage and number of trains, the trestle would probably require replacement in 25 to 30 years. After extensive studies, by 1955 a new rock causeway was begun paralleling the trestle and some 1500 feet to the north. When the new causeway fill had been completed in 1959, using more modern equipment and technology, 16 million cubic yards of mud along the lake bottom had to be excavated leaving a trench into which were dumped over 45.5 million cubic yards of rock, sand and gravel. Ocean-going barges and tugboats had to be built elsewhere, disassembled, brought to the lake side by train, reassembled and put to work moving and dumping the material into the required locations.

Since 1959, the original trestle has stood abandoned, a quarter-mile away from the causeway. Only in 1996 have some companies been authorized to remove the pilings and deck timbers, much of which have been recycled into other purposes, such as building timbers and furniture.

In the painting for this chapter, Southern Pacific GP9 #3769, in the original black with silver, red and orange trim, affectionately called the "Black Widow" paint scheme, heads a manifest freight eastward across the Lucin Cutoff's Great Salt Lake trestle in 1957. During the 1960's, Southern Pacific changed the paint livery on its locomotives to the dark gray with red ends. This diesel locomotive now resides at the Utah State Railroad Museum in the most recent color scheme.

BLACK WIDOWS ON THE LAKE

Watercolor 17" x 24" 1997

One of the greatest engineering marvels of the 20th century has been Southern Pacific's trestle across the Great Salt Lake. The original rail line skirted the north of the lake where steep grades made the running difficult and slow. In 1904 the trestle was completed and with it, a faster schedule from Ogden to California's Bay area.

In the mid-1970's I witnessed the Southern Pacific extension across the lake. Although the trestle had been replaced by a fill, it was something that everyone should see. While I was there, three or four trains came by. On the fill from Ogden to Promontory Point the trains would run at 60 mph; from Promontory Point across the long side of the lake to Lucin, the speed dropped considerably.

When asked to paint something on the trestle in the lake, many ideas came to mind. I had first thought of a passenger train at night with the lights of the train reflecting off the lake and the lights from Ogden in the background. A full moon with the snows of the Wasatch silhouetted against a clear night sky completed my image.

Bob Geier suggested doing one of Southern Pacific's *Daylight* colored 4-8-4s coming across the lake at sunset. It was also suggested that one of SP's Cab-forwards be posed on the lake with a freight drag. All great ideas and I hope that someone will commission me to do them in the future. It was also imperative that I was to paint GP-9 #3769, which was donated to the museum. The two came together and the result ended up in paint. The location is almost at Midlake with the Lakeside mountains in the back.

Although the Southern Pacific GP-9 at the museum is in the later "Bloody Nose" scheme, I wanted to do the locomotive in its first paint guise the "Black Widow." I actually hope that someday the museum will paint the GP-9 in the old colors as in this painting. I also decided to make the lash-up (the other locomotives trailing the first unit) a 1960's mix. So I added some more GP-9s and a couple of F-7 B-units. As is, this represents what happened many times a day, day after day, in the early 1960's.

Now the trestle is gone. The F-units are gone and only a few GP-9s are running as of this writing. Through painting, it is kind of nice to be able to go back in time and see how things once were.

Chapter 15

Wasatch Warrior

Union Pacific Railroad in Weber Canyon
1964

As the steam era came to an end, Union Pacific utilized a variety of existing stock diesel-electric locomotives from several manufacturers but was not totally satisfied with the need to assemble several engines together to achieve the needed horsepower to haul the long, heavy trains up Utah's Weber and Echo canyons. Working with General Electric, the railroad developed a 4500 hp gas turbine locomotive that could pull a typical, for the time, 4400-ton freight train up through the canyons, replacing up to three conventional diesel engines. In fact, with Utah's relatively high elevation and often cold winters, these turbines were found to be more efficient than where they were constructed closer to sea level.

Pleased with this locomotive, Union Pacific and General Electric designed an even more powerful gas turbine, rated at 8500 hp, subsequently increased to 10,000 hp, making it the most powerful locomotive on earth. This new two-unit locomotive was permanently coupled together and weighed 849,248 pounds (424.6 tons), and could move at speeds up to 65 mph on level terrain. The lead unit contained the engineer's cab, electrical cabinets, dynamic brake resistors and an 850 hp diesel engine that was

needed to start the turbine. The second unit contained the single-shaft turbine itself and two 3500 hp generators that powered the locomotive's motors. The total length including the fuel-oil tender was 179 feet.

The most difficult portion of the original transcontinental railroad constructed by Union Pacific in 1868-69 was between Evanston, Wyoming, and Ogden, Utah. Grades in the canyons were steep and the civil engineers had all they could do to keep the railbeds at a grade that was commensurate with good railroad construction and operation. Maximum grades in Echo Canyon reached 1.77 percent. Helper engines were oftentimes needed to get a train up the hill. Locomotives such as the Big Boy steam engines and these gas turbines often could handle the job by themselves, which saved the railroad from having to use two or three engine crews.

However, as dispatchers continued to send out longer and heavier trains, smaller, regular-type diesel locomotives would also be assigned. These "helper" engines would be electrically hooked up, along with the air brake system, so that they could be controlled from the lead engine. This multiple-unit operation saved money over steam helpers by not requiring an extra engine crew that the steamers were required to have. As with the Big Boys, the gas turbines were specifically built for the steep Wasatch Mountain grades and over the Continental Divide to Cheyenne, Wyoming.

In 1916, Union Pacific had discovered that with the steep grades in the canyons, trains were getting bogged down and were creating a bottleneck in the system. The answer was to increase capacity by adding a second mainline track up the canyon. This had already been done on several portions on the eastern flatter segments of the system and was effective in speeding merchandise and passengers as requested by shipping companies and the traveling public.

The steepest section, from Emory to Wahsatch (the town of Wahsatch is spelled with an 'h', the mountain range without) at the summit of the canyon, was built from 1916-17 and required the drilling of four new tunnels in order to maintain a grade of not greater than 1.14 percent. Because most of the original transcontinental line had been constructed away from the mountainside, the new track was usually built against the mountains, necessitating the boring of the tunnels. Also, because of tunnel construction and the need to keep grades at 1.14 percent or lower, the new line crossed under the original line at Curvo, deep in North Echo Canyon, four miles west of Wahsatch. To be as efficient as possible, the new line with its consistently lower grades was designated as the eastbound, uphill track; the original track with steeper grades is the downhill one. And while ordinarily the Union Pacific operates its trains on double track using right-hand running, similar to regular automobile traffic, this stretch of the railroad, between Ogden and Curvo, due to the grade-separated crossing, requires left-hand running. Only during the few times when track work is being performed in the canyon will a train be seen running in the opposite direction from that specified. At practically all locations in Weber Canyon and most in Echo Canyon the two tracks are quite close to each other; but in the upper half of Echo Canyon, the two lines may be as much as a quarter-mile apart from each other due to the gradient required on the 1916 track.

Other sections of the canyons were double-tracked in the next few years, resulting in the boring of still three more tunnels in Weber Canyon, so that by 1926, the entire canyon territory from Ogden to way east of Evanston was complete and traffic was running more smoothly than ever. These jobs added to the already expensive railroad construction from the plains of Wyoming to the Great Basin of Utah and of running the railroad. But of course work that had to be done to keep the Union Pacific as efficient and productive as possible.

Interestingly enough, when all the tunnels were cut in these canyons, they were built high enough in the first place that they have been able to accommodate the modern extra-tall freight cars, such as automobile carriers and the double-stack containers that provide so much of Union Pacific's tonnage. None of them have had to be enlarged. In contrast, most tunnels on other railroads, even those of the Southern Pacific over Donner Pass, have had to be enlarged or circumvented in recent years.

This view of locomotive #26, pulling train Extra-26 in 1967, is eastbound in Weber Canyon just east of Taggart. The "X" in the train number window meant that the train was an extra, a freight. The practice of using the "X" was dropped in the 1970's when the railroads generally quit running passenger trains. The rear of this solid train of refrigerator cars from the West Coast bound for markets on the Eastern seaboard is still inside the bore of Tunnel #8. Cold winters at higher elevations improved the efficiency of the gas turbine locomotives. The train is making approximately 28 mph.

This magnificent locomotive is one of only three known to be still in existence. Originally sold to Continental Leasing Corp. in 1971, the engine is one of the prime exhibition pieces on display at the Utah State Railroad Museum.

WASATCH WARRIOR

Watercolor 18" x 27" 1995

The first painting I did for this book was to be the cover. I am glad it made it on the inside also. For this painting Bob wanted me to do Turbine #26, which is on display at the museum, as it was in service. I had no stipulations other than it had to be in Utah and that it be in watercolor. Hot dawg, I couldn't wait to start it! Painting a turbine is nothing new to me. I had painted many of these locomotives and didn't want to do something I had previously rendered. I would have chosen Echo Canyon, but, in watercolor, Echo's rock walls are difficult to capture. Plus I have done that many times already. I thought of putting it in the depths of Weber Canyon, where the Big Boy is rendered in this book but decided against it. So, I did the next best thing—a road trip. Anywhere on the line between Ogden and Wahsatch is scenic, so anyplace I would choose would work. I turned off the exit at Taggart, Utah, and took the old road as far as I could go. There it was, the scene I was looking for. One problem is that when I-84 was built, it changed the scenery. In fact, I was standing under the freeway when I found the spot. Lucky for me, a photograph was taken of this area in 1945. I used that to back-date the scene and, voila, just like magic!

The Union Pacific, always searching for new and better power, spawned the 4-6-6-4 and 4-8-8-4 for the run between Ogden, Utah, and Green River, Wyoming. In the 1950's UP's huge 4-8-8-4's were 10 years old and something new was needed to replace them when and if the 4-8-8-4 was going to give out. The answer was with the Gas Turbine Electric Locomotive (GTEL). Instead of a diesel engine inside a locomotive to turn the generator, General Electric put in a jet engine (turbine). The fuel used at the time was waste oil, so expense of running these beasts would not be excessive.

The culmination of the Gas Turbine locomotive came in 1958 with the first three-unit "Big Blow" as they became known. Number 26 was built in February 1961 and retired in February 1970. The locomotive was built to deliver 8,500 hp but under cold conditions at high altitudes could develop 10,000 hp. The length of the three-unit turbine was 178 feet 11 3/4 inches It weighed 849,248 pounds without tender and had a top speed of 65 mph. It became "world's most powerful locomotive" with a tractive effort of 212, 312 pounds When retired, #26 had accumulated 1,007,853 miles, most of which were accrued between Salt Lake City, Utah, and Green River, Wyoming.

The GTEL became the top line of motive power in the late 1950's and early 1960's relieving the 4-8-8-4 as the main power out of Ogden. The turbines, too, would go the way of the steam locomotive, as in 1969 the "Centennial" DDA-40X would start replacing them on Union Pacific's main trains.

I love those turbines! I am glad that at least one is on display in Ogden. These were fabulous locomotives and always make for great paintings. Yes, I like this painting. Do you think the museum will let me buy it back?

Chapter 16

Big Hook

Union Pacific at Emory, Utah
1968

The Big Hook. That is the affectionate name that railroaders give to the railway crane. These cranes are manufactured in a number of sizes, weights and from 25-ton to 250-ton capacities.

Cranes can be used in many situations, depending on the size of the work to be done. The most common usages are in bridge construction where huge steel girders have to be lifted and set in place on their footings, and to sort through collisions and derailments, picking up locomotives and cars. They also are equipped with a variety of cable sizes and strengths, again, depending on the expected usages. Although transported behind (or pushed to a particular site as need may be) by one of the railroad's regular freight locomotives, these behemoths have a diesel engine that can propel themselves forward or backward at just a very few miles per hour (actually feet per minute) as they are positioned for their work.

They are always accompanied by several support cars in the work train, from boxcars full of cable, chains, huge wooden blocks, welding supplies and various crates of bolts, spikes, clamps, etc., to flat cars carrying extra wheels, lengths of rail and other large pieces of equipment and repair materials as well as huge battery- or diesel-operated spotlights. Such a flat car also serves as a "spacer" car over which the large boom of the crane rides so as to not intrude on a taller car or engine. A typical work train would also carry an office (command) car, usually a rebuilt passenger car, rather than a smaller caboose that would not have sufficient internal capacity for all the office machines, records and associated officials and clerks. One or more dormitory cars would be included in order to provide bunks and lounge areas for the small army of trained workers. Railroad construction and repair is usually a 24-hour operation so as to get the piece of railroad under consideration opened up as soon as possible. Two or three crews would interchange with each other, so sleeping facilities and rest locations are important. Special heater cars are often included during winter repair work. The work force would need to be fed, so there is also a commissary and kitchen car assigned with a complement of cooks and kitchen help. Because this is rough work, the kitchen car would not be confused with a dining car on a passenger train although such a car may have been converted from a former diner.

As with many other features of railroading, the major piece of equipment is the most prominent aspect of the scene, train, activity, etc., but the most important part of crane activity has to do with the many people involved. Railroad construction and maintenance is often quite specialized requiring specific skills and knowledge. Often, these specially trained people are sent from place to place around the whole railroad system to utilize their expertise to the fullest extent.

In the event of a derailment of a heavy locomotive, often two cranes would be sent in from both directions to right the errant engine and place it back on the rails. This requires extending the crane's outriggers onto the track bed and placing the boom where the cables needed to retrieve the object could be looped around the crane's hook. In some cases, besides using the outriggers, the crane would be clamped to the rail, partly to keep it from tipping over with a heavy weight hanging from the boom, and also to help the crane obtain better leverage. In extremely remote locations, a detour or passing siding might have to be installed next to the main track in order to best utilize all the equipment on hand.

The crane's large hook itself is never used to pull an engine or car directly, but is employed to tie onto the strong cables that would be strung around the item. This is where the multitude of workers comes in Cables and chains need to be rigged up to the engine or car in such a manner that the work can be accomplished as quickly as possible with the safety for all involved as prime concern. Spreader bars are usually employed to attach the cables so as to equalize the forces and stresses on the equipment and to keep from damaging a derailed piece of equipment or rolling stock any more than necessary.

In the case where an engine or car has tumbled a hundred feet or so down a steep embankment on a high fill, the coordination of the directing official, the dozens of workers on the ground and the crane operators approaches extensive cooperative efforts and logistics. Each crane's capacity as well as that of the cables used has to be calculated with great accuracy.

Many smaller capacity cranes were constructed to utilize just one large hook. The largest cranes usually had two hooks. The main hook of the largest cranes is deployed from the center of the boom, while a smaller hook is located at the boom tip. The hooks and associated boom cables are designed to be operated independently so the crane operator and his assistant have to be really nimble and constantly watchful as they deal with the numerous levers, gauges, handles and knobs in the control cab.

The painting depicts Union Pacific crane #X250, along with a similar capacity mate replacing a turnout complete with crossties spiked to the rails at Emory, a former track gang village part way up Echo Canyon. The switch complex was built elsewhere and transported to the site on one or more flatcars; and, although the turnout only weighs a few dozen tons, well under the crane's capacity, because it is some 60-70 feet in length, it required two cranes to manipulate the awkwardly-shaped piece of equipment.

Shown also here is a portion of the double ground work force required to perform all the rigging, bolting and attaching while the cranes' booms lift, hold, set and secure the track sections firmly in place. The supervisors and foremen are wearing the white hard hats; the general laborers the yellow ones.

Durbano Salvage graciously donated this Big Hook to the Utah State Railroad Museum where it can be seen and examined up close. The crane's number, X250 just coincidentally happens to be Union Pacific's number on this 250-ton machine. One can see from all the controls in the cab how the operator would have to be expertly trained in the myriad of details concerned with the crane's proper and safe operation.

BIG HOOK

Watercolor 18"x 24" 1997

When I was told to paint the 250-ton crane the museum has, I was not too thrilled. Finding photos of these machines at work are not too prevalent, almost non-existent. As with all things, sometimes things go wrong. As such, usually a company will purchase something to clean up a mess, in case one happens. For this painting I had visions of a derailment, not too good for a pro-railroad book and even worse to paint.

As I thought about it I knew that these cranes were used for more than just putting things back on the track. Again to the library to do research. Anything that can raise something that weighs 250 tons could pick up lots of things. I bet that those who operated these things thought that too. I could see them sitting on a siding, waiting in the hot sun for a few trains to clear, hooking up that big hook to an old shack and taking it for a drag. In my search, I found an old New York Central photograph of a "big hook" replacing a section of panel track. I thought to myself, this will work! I chose an area on the Union Pacific that had some scenery and triple track to make this plausible.

I chose the siding at Emory, Utah, on the busy transcontinental route. I had thoughts of putting a train inching its way up the open track but the way the crane is situated, it would have been fouling the mainline. Instead I added a small army of track workers. I also threw in a few workers to lean on their shovels. To pose for these workers I used one of the shovel-leaning gangs that work for the state road department doing what they do best—shovel-leaning! With that remark, I guess the road in front of my house will never be resurfaced in my lifetime. I, too, put in one of the UP's signal bridges painted in that ugly green they used until the mid 1970's. They now paint these bridges silver (thank heavens).

This painting has a lot of human interest and I must admit that once under way it was fun to paint. However, as I look at it I think this would have been better with one of Union Pacific's big turbines or 4-8-8-4s running through here sans the crane!

Chapter 17

Storming Through the Castle Gates
Utah Railway in the Price River Canyon
1976

When the Mormon pioneers settled in the Salt Lake Valley, the early leaders issued a call for them to discover and exploit commercial coal deposits. In 1854, the territorial legislature even provided an award of $1000, a hefty sum in those days, to the person or group who first located such a deposit within 40 miles of Salt Lake City. Four years later, suitable coal deposits up to 10 feet thick were found in northern Utah near the Weber River. The city of Coalville was established and the territory was in the coal business. After a decade of delivering the mineral by wagon load, once the Union Pacific came down nearby Echo and Weber canyons in 1869, the coal could be delivered to the Salt Lake Valley much more expeditiously, although somewhat more costly. The Summit County Railroad was then formed to take the coal from the mines to the Union Pacific at the town of Echo. With subsequent population increases and demand for the product, these original sources were found to be inadequate.

Then in 1875, more coal was discovered in the Pleasant Valley area of eastern Utah. This appeared to be even more promising than the Weber River deposits in terms of vein thickness, quality and availability. Mines were opened and production began in earnest, but here again, transportation was a problem. It was partially solved by the construction of the three-foot gauge Utah & Pleasant Valley Railroad that took the coal-laden gondolas from Winter Quarters to Springville. These new mines kept up with the demand for a time, but still more coal to be delivered faster was needed.

About that time, in 1882, as the narrow gauge D&RGW Railway was building westward from the Colorado line, when construction crews cut into various hills and cliffsides in the Castle Gate region, they unearthed several more potentially valuable and workable high-grade coal veins. This resulted in the real formation of Utah's "Coal Boom", which lasted clear into the 1950's.

After the D&RGW Railroad was formed subsequent to the standard-gauging of the earlier Railway and merging with the Rio Grande Western Railway, the big coal-carrying gondola cars were admirably suited to the transportation of large amounts of coal to wherever it was needed. By the turn of the century, there were dozens of huge coal-fired industries in the Salt Lake Valley, particularly ore stamp mills and smelters. In fact, the Valley in 1900 possessed more non-ferrous smelters than anywhere else on earth. And almost every one of them required coal with which to operate.

With this pressing need, a couple of small coal-hauling railroads were built from the expansive coal fields east of the Colorado Plateau in Carbon and Emery counties. These railroads had to run eastward to Price, then back westward, and too much revenue was taken up by the extra miles and time involved.

The Utah Railway was then organized which took the coal

directly north from the hillside mines to the D&RGW mainline up the Price River Canyon. Due to the usual tiffs that develop when competing rail lines vie for tariffs, the Utah Railway decided to build its own line paralleling the Rio Grande. After completing a separate route from Springville to Thistle, the two roads came to an understanding and double-tracked the D&RGW route from Thistle to Utah Railway Junction, just west of Helper, where the Utah swung off south toward the mines. This way, all westbound traffic of both railroads uses the Rio Grande's north track, and all eastbound trains utilize the Utah Railway's south track. Then to complicate matters further, the Utah Railway formed a consortium with the Union Pacific, Rio Grande's competitor, called the "Utah Coal Route", which owned a fleet of gondolas, and transported coal around the northern part of the state, down to the iron mines on Union Pacific's line in Iron County, as well as to other western states. This company operated until the extensive demand for coal dropped off in the early 1950's.

There were several decades of diminished coal production in eastern Utah, and much of what was left was sent elsewhere. Then since the Intermountain Power Project was completed in south-central Utah near Delta, much of the coal produced by mines along the Utah Railway has gone to that massive power plant. Dedicated trains of coal hoppers are taken directly to the plant either by the Utah Railway handing off the trains to the Union Pacific at Springville, or by the Union Pacific's locomotives themselves running all the way east to the mines.

The rail line continues as dual tracks from Utah Railway Junction to Price, of necessity, and both tracks then belonged to the D&RGW Railroad. The D&RGW was merged with the Southern Pacific in the 1980's, then in 1996, the Southern Pacific was merged into the Union Pacific. Even the corporate headquarters of the Utah Railway were moved from Salt Lake City to Martin where the operation and maintenance offices and main yard facilities are located, just up the hill from Helper.

The Utah Railway owned a variety of motive power through the years, beginning with the usual steam engines, single as well as articulated. In the 1950's a fleet of six-motored diesel units from ALCO was acquired, painted in a pale gray livery with a red stripe along the entire length of the locomotives. As these engines wore out, the railway had to go elsewhere for locomotives as the American Locomotive Company had gone out of business. They were replaced by an eclectic mix of diesel units from other railroads, many of which were never repainted except to remove the former owners' names. Finally, the railroad has settled on General Motor's Electro-Motive Division's six-axle SD40 type engines, with one exception, and all are painted a slightly darker gray than before with a wider red stripe.

Pictured here at Castle Gate during the 1976 transition period, leading similar units as well as an RSD4, is ALCO #401, an RSD15 type, newly acquired from the Santa Fe Railway. Still in Santa Fe's dark blue and yellow, the Utah's shop forces have replaced the Santa Fe name with "UTAH RAILWAY." When the railway changed over to an all EMD (Electro-Motive Division) fleet, this engine was purchased by a Salt Lake scrapyard, which then donated it to the Promontory Chapter of the National Railway Historical Society in Salt Lake City. It was subsequently used by a rail operation at Clive, Utah, which later gave it to the Utah State Railroad Museum where it is on display.

STORMING THROUGH THE CASTLE GATES

Oil 18"x 24" 1998

One of the best loved yet little known railroads in Utah is the Utah Railway. This railroad has been around for ages, hauling just one item—coal.

When coal was discovered in the lower Price River Canyon and in the surrounding areas of central Utah, a railroad was needed to transport it to Salt Lake City. The Denver & Rio Grande Western already had a line close to the area and had built some spurs to get to the coal deposits. The United States Smelting, Refining and Mining Corporation planned on opening mines in the area and needed a way to move vast amounts of coal. The mines of the area were already being served by the Utah Southern and the Castle Valley railroads. However, the poor quality of those railroads' track and locomotives and the amount of expected tonnage caused concern. It was decided that the USSR&M would build its own railroad from the Wasatch Plateau to Provo, Utah, and a connection with the San Pedro, Los Angeles & Salt Lake Railroad. A line paralleling the D&RGW tracks over Soldier Summit was surveyed, but in 1912 the D&RGW decided to double-track its mainline and let the Utah Railway use the trackage. In 1914 this railroad started hauling coal and has ever since. Motive power for the Utah has always been no nonsense and simple. In the steam days it used second-hand 2-8-0s and large 2-10-2s and 2-8-8-0s based on a Union Pacific design. As the railroad turned to dieselization, it chose ALCO to build diesels and design the paint scheme for its new motive power. ALCO came up with white as the main color for the locomotive and a red stripe running down the center.

As the length of trains increased, the Utah decided to get more ALCOs. In 1971 it purchased one locomotive from the Central Railroad of New Jersey. It bought two more ALCOs from the Chesapeake & Ohio in 1972 and in 1975 it picked up four more from Santa Fe. None of the new purchases would wear the white and red of the former units.

I believe this to be the finest painting in the book. It just epitomizes Utah! Here we find Utah #401 in the lead. The museum has this locomotive on display. It is an RSD 15 with 2400 hp built for the Santa Fe in 1959. Behind #401 is #402 another of the RSD 15 class, followed by #601, an 1800 hp RSD 12 built in 1956 for the Chesapeake & Ohio. Behind #601 is #301, a 1600 hp RSD 4 built for the Utah Railway in 1952. Behind that is a regular 8,000 ton coal train. Unseen around the corner are the rest of the fleet of ALCOs in mid-train helper service. I chose the lower portion of the Price River Canyon with Castle Gate in the background. Although the right tower of Castle Gate was torn down in 1966, I decided to put it in anyway—artist license.

So here I have painted a typical spring or fall day in Utah. A heavy coal train struggling up the 2.4 percent grade on its way to Provo with a light snow falling. I can just hear those Utah ALCOs as they fight with all their worth to keep this train moving. I love it!

Chapter 18

Desert Hot Shot

Union Pacific near Milford, Utah
1979

As the 19th century came to a close, numerous financial interests in the Los Angeles, California, area, including those of copper-mining magnate Senator William A. Clark of Montana, began to focus on still another transcontinental rail route to southern California. Already served by the Southern Pacific and Santa Fe railroads, it was felt that this rapidly growing locale could still enjoy further business and traffic from the central part of the Rocky Mountain West. In 1900, it was decided that the numerous rail lines in the Los Angeles basin, being merged into one system, would extend its lines all the way up to Salt Lake City as the San Pedro, Los Angeles & Salt Lake Railroad. Grades would be among the mildest and curves the easiest of all the transcontinentals. Besides, the route was 200 miles shorter from Clark's Montana mines to a deep-water seaport and would have far fewer problems with severely inclement winter weather.

Edward H. Harriman, president of the Union Pacific, however, also had been observing southern California but was involved with attempting to merge the Southern Pacific into the Union Pacific.

Harriman tried to buy out Clark using the U.P.-controlled Oregon Short Line already close to the Nevada border, but Clark was bound to build his own railroad.

In 1901, both construction forces under Clark and Harriman were building in the same tight confines of Clover Creek Canyon a short distance west of the Utah-Nevada border. However, due to a number of court battles and injunctions, construction was often interrupted with much friction and ill will being demonstrated on both sides. Both railroad companies apparently planned to build parallel, competing lines in a relatively barren and underpopulated region of the country. But then early in 1902, all construction had stopped to allow legal proceedings to occur.

Finally, in July 1902, William A. Clark and E.H. Harriman compromised, joined forces and merged their competing lines into a single, viable railroad. Through the give and take of such matters, the Oregon Short Line sold its interests from Salt Lake City southward, and the entire line from Salt Lake to the Los Angeles area took the name of the San Pedro, Los Angeles & Salt Lake Railroad. The new railroad, dubbed the "Salt Lake Route" was completed in 1905 and began to compete very well with the Santa Fe for traffic between southern California and Chicago, then to the lucrative markets in Pennsylvania and New York.

The new railroad's quite lengthy name was a real mouthful and although nicknamed the "Salt Lake Route," it quickly became referred to by the railroad workers simply as "The Pedro." Some years later as the city of San Pedro was annexed by Los Angeles to become a suburb, the first part of the railroad's name became redundant, resulting in renaming the road the Los Angeles & Salt Lake. Even today, the LA & SL is still a separate corporation within the Union Pacific system, running from Salt Lake City through Milford, Las Vegas, Nevada, and Barstow, California, through Cajon Pass, using Santa Fe Railway tracks by way of trackage rights agreements, to Los Angeles. And it is still called "The Pedro" by railroaders from Salt Lake to California.

During the Second World War years, consideration was given to upgrading the line in order to handle Union Pacific's huge Big Boy steam engines. But due to a general lack of water in the area, this idea was abandoned. In fact, this desolate, almost waterless route was one of the first that was completely dieselized when it became apparent that the diesel-electric locomotive was going to eventually be the means of the demise of steam railroading.

Union Pacific, although still buying new steam locomotives in the 1940's, nonetheless could see the benefits of diesel-electric locomotion and tried numerous models from all the major locomotive builders. It became an operative nuisance to couple up several early smaller diesel engines in order to provide the necessary horsepower to pull its long, heavy freight trains. Turbines, although successful in certain areas, were not in others.

Union Pacific's mechanical engineers began working with those of General Motor's Electro-Motive Division and developed the world's largest and most powerful diesel locomotive. This was essentially two smaller General Purpose (GP 40) engines mounted on a single frame and riding on two four-motored traction trucks. Although a precursor model using the eight axles had been produced in relatively small numbers, it developed only 5000 hp, not enough for Union Pacific's needs. This new locomotive was designed to produce 6600 hp and seemed to be just what the railroad needed. Because the unit was really two locomotives in

one, both engines were inspected and overhauled at the same time. The railroad was aware that occasionally, one of the two parts may have had to be repaired even though the other one didn't. The hope was that it wouldn't be too often, as that would be the equivalent of shutting down an otherwise operable locomotive while repairing the first. This problem did appear more often than the railroad's maintenance facilities preferred and possibly this is why only 47 of these locomotives were constructed, all for Union Pacific.

The first several of these huge, almost 100-foot long locomotives in the model series DDA40X were completed in early 1969 and were named the Centennial type and numbered in the 6900 class in honor of the completion of the Union Pacific and the centennial of the Golden Spike ceremony at Promontory in 1869. The "DD" refers to the two four-axle trucks under the locomotive, the "A" means it is an A-unit, one with a cab for operation. There were no B-units made as there were for the DD35 series. Because of the gear ratio of these engines, they generally ran only with each other, or with a re-geared series of SD40 locomotives, renumbered into a new 8000 series. Although built as freight locomotives, #6900 was used at least once heading a streamlined passenger train.

Some 15 of these behemoths still survive, one of which, #6916, shares the outdoor display area with the Union Pacific turbine at the Ogden Union Station museum. The Union Pacific Railroad still uses #6936, based in Cheyenne, Wyoming, on special excursions. The painting depicts Centennial #6916, along with an SD40-2 and a sister Centennial, pulling a long westbound train of highway trailers a few miles south of Milford.

DESERT HOT SHOT

Watercolor 18" x 24" 1997

One of my most vivid railroad memories was back in the summer of 1984. I was headed to Los Angeles just after finishing finals of my spring semester classes. It was a hot afternoon and I was 30 miles out of Yermo, California. As I headed down I-15, I looked in my rearview mirror and caught a glimpse of a headlight. I pulled off the road and waited for the train behind the light. As it approached, I could tell it was one of Union Pacific's "Super Van" hot shots with an honest-to-goodness 6900 on the point! It was the latter part of 1983 that the Union Pacific reactivated their 6900 fleet after it was in mothballs since 1980. To my regret I didn't have my camera, but locked in my mind are the hours I spent pacing that fantastic image of 6900 and its trailing units and train. At Barstow, I took the old Route 66 that follows the Santa Fe mainline to Victorville, CA., over which the Union Pacific has trackage rights. There I was, alone on the road with hot desert air pouring through my open windows. Adjacent to me was one of the most amazing locomotives ever built running at 70 plus mph with a mile of trailers and containers on flat cars dragging behind.

I have chased and paced many of the 6900 class locomotives all over Union Pacific's far-flung system but for some reason chasing this train through the desert on this hot afternoon stands out above the rest.

I was first acquainted with the big "Centennial" locomotives at the age of eight. It was May 10, 1969, in Ogden as the first of these magnificent locomotives backed into Ogden's Union Station. The number "6900" was chosen in celebration of the 100th anniversary of the driving of the golden spike. From the years 1969 to 1971, 47 of these huge diesel locomotives would be built, all for the Union Pacific. These were the locomotives that would replace the gas turbine as UP's front-line power.

The 6900's had a length of 98 feet-5 inches, weighed 545,432 pounds and developed 6,600 hp. Fuel capacity was 8,200 gallons and it was geared for running at 90 mph. To get an idea of its size, it weighs over five times as much as a fully-loaded Boeing 727!

Fifteen of these locomotives have been preserved, one of which still sees duty on the Union Pacific. Number 6916 now belongs to the Utah State Railroad Museum. This locomotive was one of the "Centennial" locomotives brought back from mothballs to run again in 1983. At the time of mothballing, the unit had 692,471 miles on it and after put back into duty it accumulated a few 100,000 more!

The 6900's have always been a joy for me to render. When asked to do one, I knew exactly what to paint. It would be in the desert, southern Utah with a "Super Van" running at 70 mph. In my teenage years the UP made "super sandwiches" with two 6900s and an 8000 class SD-40-2 regeared for 90 mph service. So I give you Desert Hot Shot, more of a memory to me than any other painting in this book. Oh, to be track-side once again to see these locomotives doing what they did best—run!.

Chapter 19

Big Macs and Double Stacks
Union Pacific at Soldier Summit
1999

Time marches on. In the 130 plus years since the arrival of the first train in Utah Territory, the mountains and valleys have witnessed many changes. After the completion of the transcontinental rail line in northern Utah, tracks began to penetrate most inhabited parts of the territory. By 1896 when Utah became the 45th state in the Union, rail lines had spread like a spider web into valuable farming areas as well as to rich silver, gold and copper mines. Freight trains grew from 20 to 30 cars of 36-40 feet to today's trains that exceed a mile in length with more than 100 cars, each with an average length of 50 feet. Some trains consist solely of 100 automobile racks, each 89-feet long.

Passenger trains flourished from 1920 to 1960, with the major depots in the state hosting up to 10 trains a day in each direction. These days, with autos at everyone's disposal and airplanes carrying business travelers as well as tourists to far-flung destinations, a single Amtrak passenger train in each direction east and west passes through Salt Lake City at very inconvenient times. Ogden, the former "Junction City," no longer sees any passenger train activity at all. The Heber Valley Railroad, Utah's only steam-powered short-line tourist-excursion railway, running on a land-locked remnant of the D&RGW between Heber City and Provo Canyon, hauls about as many passengers as does Amtrak in the state. The newly-constructed light-rail passenger line, TRAX, short for Transit Express, carries many business people as well as shoppers between Sandy and Salt Lake City; and commuter trains between the Provo/Springville and Brigham City/Ogden areas are under consideration for carrying many people just when passenger traffic appeared to be the bleakest. With the Interstate and other highways and roads through the most densely populated areas becoming so congested, many thousands of local travelers have found that it makes much more sense to take the light-rail or commuter trains and not have to worry about the travails of highway travel.

At one point, around the early 1900's, there were over a hundred railroad companies in the state. During the last century, many have been abandoned for various reasons, such as the loss of business or redundant trackage. Many others have been merged into larger systems. Rail consolidation began in earnest in 1981 when the Union Pacific bought up the Western Pacific turning it into the Feather River Division of the U.P. In the 1990's, the Denver & Rio Grande Western merged with the Southern Pacific with the S.P. name remaining. In 1996, Union Pacific bought up the Southern Pacific and Utah essentially became a one-railroad state. The federal government made certain that competition would exist for the many industries that rely upon rail transportation by allowing the Burlington Northern & Santa Fe Railroad to have access to all the industries that had previously been handled by Southern Pacific. Besides the far-reaching Union Pacific system, only a small handful of shortline feeder or switching railroads are left, namely the Salt Lake, Garfield & Western and Salt Lake City Southern railroads in Salt Lake City, the Utah Central Railway in Ogden, and the Utah Railway between Utah's coal fields and Provo; along with just four industrial lines serving a single industry, such as the Kennecott Mining Railroad in Salt Lake County, the Deseret Western in Uintah County, the Intermountain Power Plant in Millard County and the Geneva Steel Company's operation below Orem.

Railroading is still a big business, however, not only in Utah but throughout the nation. Since railroads have been deregulated by the federal government so as to be more competitive with trucks and barges, rail activity has gone from its lowest point in terms of amount of tonnage carried per mile of track to a major growth industry. Where many railroads across the country down-sized their operations by pulling up supposedly unneeded trackage, they now are wishing they had left the rails in place in order to handle the increase in traffic.

Much of the marked increase has come through more modern methods of transportation. No longer are 40-foot boxcars seen in freight trains. Fifty-footers are now the norm with many even longer. Many trains carry only one commodity, such as coal, grain, chemicals, cement and automobiles. Even the formerly ubiquitous general manifest freight is not likely to be the first train one sees when passing a train along a highway.

In the 1980's several overseas shipping companies that ship freight between the Far East and Europe determined that it was cheaper and faster to put their freight in steel containers and transload them to trains running between the coasts of North America (the United States and Canada) than it was to take the long and tedious route through the Panama Canal. Since then, not only has the former ocean-going freight traveled overland,

but thousands of companies, including United Parcel Service and the United States Post Office, find the container business to be more than adequate for their inter-city needs. Special cars have been constructed with low-slung "wells" between the truck wheels of the cars so that the containers ride just a few inches above the rail height. This allows another container to be carried on top of the lower one, thereby doubling the capacity of a train. Containers of 40, 45, 48 and 53 feet in length can be carried in a train using any number of well cars, some with single well capacity, most with five articulated wells per car. Although the railroads in other states have had to reconfigure many of their tunnels to accept the extreme height of 19 feet of these double-stacked containers, none of Utah's tunnels have had to be modified. This intermodal business (using more than one mode of travel) has substantially helped to bring rail freight operations into acceptable prosperity in the 1990's and beyond.

Modern locomotives have kept up with the demand for more horsepower. Both General Electric and General Motor's Electro-Motive Division continue to expand their research to provide more and more horsepower in more efficient and reliable locomotives. The painting for this chapter shows a typical double-stack train in 1999 after the recent mergers of the Union Pacific with the Southern Pacific and Chicago & North Western, led by a new SD90MAC locomotive, developing 6000 hp and utilizing Alternating Current electrical motors. The train is heading for the highest mainline railroad location in Utah, the 7440-foot elevation at Soldier Summit.

BIG MACS AND DOUBLE STACKS

Oil 18" x 24" 1998

As time progresses so do the railroads. The Denver & Rio Grande Western, Western Pacific and Southern Pacific have been swallowed up by Union Pacific. Some say this is good others say it is bad. The railroads are there for one reason—service. The amount of goods shipped via railroad is staggering. Take a look at this painting. Behind the locomotives are double stacks, or two containers or truck trailers stacked upon each other on one car. The railcar has changed over the years also. The double stack car has five wells for handling ten 40-, 45-, 48-, or 53- foot containers or twenty 20-foot containers on one set of cars. Trains of this kind can be to lengths of 7,000 to 8,000 feet and carry the equivalent of what 250 tractor trailers would be carrying on the roads! The caboose has changed also. There isn't one. Instead there is a small computer that hangs on the last coupler that sends signals to the locomotive's computer. Up front there is a two person crew who will guide this train some 286 miles and there, another crew will take the train to its next stop. All this has been done to increase service for the customer.

I was asked once in high school why railroads are important? My reply was "Do you have a car." The answer was "Yes". I asked, "How much did you pay for it?" The answer was "Too much." I then asked "Who made the car?" It was one of the big three. I then asked: Who shipped the car? Who shipped the raw materials to build the components for the car? Who supplied the material for the energy to the factory? Were there parts of the car that had been preassembled, such as radios, tires, eight—track tapes (it was during the 1970's) sub-assemblies, etc.? "And how did they all get to the factory," I asked. I also explained that for a train load of goods to be handled by any other means of transportation would have increased the price of her car by a significant factor. She then started to understand what the railroads do.

For this painting I projected a little into the future. I will say it is late spring. The location is on Soldier Summit above the Gilluly loops. While the double stacks have been around since the early 1980's and the caboose has been gone since the mid to late 1980's, the locomotive technology has improved. The three locomotives on the point have all the latest in gadgets. Computers now calculate if the rail is wet, if all the units are working and if they don't need to are put in idle to save fuel. All three locomotives are using alternating current. The lead unit #8507 is the latest from Electro-Motive Division of General Motors designated an SD-90 MAC. It has 6,000 hp with a two cycle 20 cylinder engine. The computer makes sure that the wheels don't slip. The new truck is of a radial design and steers through curves increasing traction while deceasing track and wheel wear. The two locomotives behind built by General Electric are AC- powered also and have 4,400 hp each. These too are marvelous machines. As the railroads head into the next century, speed and efficiency will be paramount.

Chapter 20

Echoes of Thunder

Union Pacific in Echo Canyon
1958

Appropriately, we conclude an art book of Utah railroading with a painting of a Union Pacific caboose trailing behind a 4-6-6-4 Challenger-type locomotive that has been assigned as a pusher, helping the regular locomotive get a long, heavy freight up the steep and demanding Weber/Echo canyon complex.

The need for pusher, or helper, engines on steep mountain grades became apparent when the requirements of a consuming nation for more commodities faster evolved before larger, more powerful locomotives could be engineered and developed. Some notable railroads in the East that utilized helper engines were the Pennsylvania and the Baltimore & Ohio. Those in the West included Union Pacific, Denver & Rio Grande Western, Southern Pacific and Western Pacific. In fact, the town of Helper, Utah, was so named because the D&RGW attached helper locomotives to most of its heavy westbound trains in order to climb over 7440-foot Soldier Summit.

These additional engines could be coupled anywhere in the train: sometimes they were placed in front of the regular 'road' locomotive, sometimes in the middle of the train and quite often on the rear end. Furthermore, depending on the length and weight of a train, more than one helper might be needed for a specific mountain grade. Photos in some books on Utah railroading even show as many as five steam engines, four in front and one pushing, on as short as a 10-car passenger train on the original 4 percent grade over Soldier Summit, before it was reduced to 2 percent by the addition of several extra miles of looping track.

In the days of steam operation, it was quite a trick to maintain the proper power produced by two or more engines in order to get and keep a train moving without either using too much force at the front end and pulling couplers apart (which happened all too frequently) or too much power from a pusher engine that might force a car to the point of a derailment (which also happened periodically). Each locomotive required a separate crew working together using whistle signals to let each other know what was required and what was happening.

Modern-day railroading still uses helpers and, although the operation is still not without stress and potential problems, it is much easier than in the steam days. One engineer, using multiple-unit electrical cabling for all the front locomotives and radio control for any mid-train or end-of-train helpers, has much better control and can handle a 10,000-ton train all by himself.

As shown in the painting, and even up until cabooses were no longer used in mainline service, the pusher engine was generally cut in just in front of the caboose. Originally, cabooses were built with wooden frames and center sills that often would snap when too much force was applied against it by a pusher engine. Even when cabooses were constructed of steel, they were still the lightest car on the train and might easily be pushed up or to one side by a strong engine behind and slip off the rail endangering the rear-end crew, damaging the caboose and delaying the trains.

In the early- to mid-20th century, it might take a whole 8 to 12-hour shift for a train crew, especially with helpers, to get a train from Ogden up to Green River, Wyoming. The train might run only at 15 to 20 mph up the steep canyons, then would have to stop at Echo and Evanston for all the engines to take on water. The locomotive might also take on coal at Evanston, and to be oiled and greased, at times taking 30 minutes or more per engine.

In the early days of railroading, once a train was of sufficient length that the engine (head-end) crew could no longer monitor the trailing cars adequately and where inordinate amounts of walking had to be done by conductors and brakemen during switching procedures, the need for a crew car at the end of the train became apparent. Originally, a flatcar with some seats or benches installed served the purpose, however, as one can imagine, this would not have been a pleasant place during inclement weather.

The next phase was for a resourceful conductor to commandeer an unused boxcar in order to keep out of the weather and to keep track of the increasing amount of paperwork. Problems with freight cars toward the rear of the train caused serious breakdowns that possibly could have been avoided if they had been spotted by the rear-end crew had they been looking. It became obvious that a special car was required for the variety of needs that were being experienced. Hence, the caboose was developed in the middle 1800's. Despite modernization of the car, the basic shape and design has changed but little since its introduction.

The caboose was the office of the conductor where he sorted the various waybills so as to know when to drop certain cars off, and when and where to pick others up. The cupola on top al-lowed the crew to observe for any problems ahead of them in the train that may not be noticeable to the engine crew. Some railways, noticeably the Southern Pacific, Western Pacific and Carbon County railroads in Utah, along with the Milwaukee Road and Kansas City Southern, utilized a type of caboose with a bay window on each side instead of the usual cupola on top. This style originated due to the tight overhead clearances on some of the eastern railroads and subsequently caught on with other lines even those which were not concerned about such clearance problems.

The caboose (or crummy, hack, way car, cabin, etc., as it was known colloquially on different railroads) was also home away from home for the conductor and one or two brakemen assigned to the train. A stove provided heat in the cool times of the year as well as for cooking meals while on the road. Bunks were available for tired trainmen in between duties. A washroom, refrigerator and lavatory were included, and even showers in more modern cabooses.

Cabooses have generally given way to more advanced technology on modern freight trains, such as the Flashing Rear End Device (FRED), but they will always hold a spot in the heart of any older railroader or trackside observer.

The caboose depicted, a CA-1 wooden type built in 1921, was utilized by Union Pacific until and even after the first steel cabooses were built for the railroad in 1942. This caboose is on display at the Utah State Railroad Museum, as are the two Wilson Meat Company cars shown in the painting.

ECHOES OF THUNDER

Oil 18"x 24" 1997

For the last painting of this book, Bob wanted a rendering of the CA-1 caboose that the museum has. I thought of just putting it on the back of some train in a bucolic setting, but that wouldn't fit with all the big power previously in the book. In fact, it would be boring!

Ever since the building of the transcontinental railroad, helpers have been used out of Ogden. In the days of steam, the 2-8-0, 2-8-2 and 2-10-2 helpers were among the regulars that would help any of a number of larger locomotives up Weber and Echo Canyons. However, the most remembered of the helpers were Union Pacific's huge 4-6-6-4 locomotives. The locomotives used out of Ogden were built for passenger service in Oregon's Blue Mountains as well as running passengers from Salt Lake City to Los Angeles. As the diesel invaded the dry Southwest desert and densely forested Northwest, the Challengers were bumped east. Most of the high stepping 4-6-6-4s ran east out of Cheyenne with long freights where their power and speed were greatly appreciated by crews. Although the diesels ran there also, the 4-6-6-4 could run between Cheyenne, Wyoming, and North Platte, Nebraska, in less time. As a result, most of the diesels working there were moved to other parts of the system.

A batch of the oil-burning 4-6-6-4s came west to Ogden while the coal burners ran out of Cheyenne. To keep the oil and coal burners separate, the oil burners were given 3700 numbers while the coal burners kept their 3800 and 3900 series numbers. Numbers 3700-3717 worked out of Ogden from 1953 to 1959. They increased the speed of any train going east dramatically. The 4-6-6-4s were usually assigned to hot shots behind the gas turbines as well as the new diesel electrics. During this time the 4-8-8-4 "Big Boys" were also being run out of Ogden, so it is possible that a 4-8-8-4 pulling on the point and a 4-6-6-4 pushing on the rear was a daily occurrence. Some question why locomotives built for running at 70 plus mph in passenger and fast freight service were used in the helper pool. To me it is all mathematical. If you have 65 miles of uphill grade, 60 eastbound freight trains, plus passenger and mail trains with set schedules, one would want to get a train over this stretch of railroad as fast as possible. Hence with a 4-6-6-4 shoving on the end, a 4,000 or 5,000 ton train would run at 45-50 mph uphill! This would keep everything on the railroad fluid! In the East, where the grades were under 20 miles in length, and the volume of passenger traffic was not as concentrated as on the UP, plodding slow helpers that ran trains at 15 mph or slower could be used. Not so on the Union Pacific.

For this painting I chose my beloved Echo Canyon, #3712 and CA-1 2624, the caboose in the museum. The year is 1958 in early summer. Up front some 80 cars away, a turbine leads the charge through the twisting canyon. I envy those who saw this in person. To those of you who witnessed these marvelous machines at work, I hope the paintings in this book rekindle fond times and memories as well as tell the importance the railroads have played through history.

Acknowledgments

Many thanks to the individuals, groups and entities listed below for the
generous contributions which helped make this book possible.

Ogden City Corporation
George S. and Dolores Dore Eccles Foundation
Ben Day, Coca Cola Bottling Company of Ogden
Dr. W. C. Swanson Family Foundation
Hostlers Model Railroaders
Annie Taylor Dee Foundation
Union Station Conductors
Jean Pell
John Bennett
Jones Family Charitable Trust
Junior E. and Blance B. Rich Foundation
Valeen Glasmann
John A. Lindquist
Leon and Judy Jones in memory of Mrs. Barbara Kimball Browning
Lucia Browning
State of Utah, Museum Services
Robert Geier in memory of Karen Mayhew
Lucia Browning in memory of Karen Mayhew and Max Wilson
Weber State University Printing Service

A special thanks to Louise Kingsbury who donated her expertise and time to edit this volume
and to Roberta Beverly for her tireless efforts in overseeing and guiding this project to completion.

A Short History of Ogden's Union Stations

The Ogden Union Station deserves it's place on the National Register of Historic Sites for the past service during the days of railroad travel and it's new role as a multipurpose community center and Museum. Ogden has in fact had three different stations since Union Pacific track crews entered the city on March 8, 1869, on their way toward Promontory Summit and the historical meeting with the Central Pacific to complete the nations first Transcontinental Railroad.

The first station was opened in November of 1869 along the right of way at the foot of 4th Street (now 24th Street) just west of Wall Avenue. This land had been donated to the Union Pacific Railroad by Brigham Young thereby ensuring that Ogden, not the Gentile stronghold of Corinne, would become Junction City. The building was a typical early depot: two stories high, of wooden frame construction, and painted a gaudy red. The boardwalk kept pedestrians out of the mud as they walked to nearby hotels, cafes, saloons, bakeries, curio ships, and other establishments catering to travelers.

As railroad traffic through Ogden increased, so did demands for a better Depot. The people of Ogden complained that the old station gave visitors a negative impression of their city. Subsequently the Ogden Union Railroad and Depot Company, a company jointly owned by the Union Pacific and the Central Pacific which had been organized to operate the Station and rail yards, agreed to build a new station. Henry Van Brunt, a friend of U. P. President Charles Adams, was selected as architect.

The cornerstone of the second station was laid November 5, 1888 at Wall Avenue and 5th Street, now 25th Street. Mayor David Eccles proclaimed a holiday. Bars closed for the afternoon and a crowd of more than 5000 braved a light snowstorm to hear Attorney Parley L. Williams deliver the keynote address. He declared "this structure now begun will in years to come offer it's hospitable roof to travelers from all lands and will be a medium through which strangers within your gates will receive their inspiration of your people, your city and your country".

The Ogden Standard described the new station as "a symbol of the dawn of the bright days of prosperity from this time is assured to Ogden, the most promising city in the West".

The structure had two story north and south wings and the three story center section that included more than 30 hotel rooms. A large electric clock donated by Ogden jeweler J. S. Lewis, was installed in the tower below an elaborate weather vane. The waiting room, ticket windows, and a cafe were on the main floor with railroad offices filling the second level.

The second Station, which went into operation early in 1889, served admirably for thirty-four years, until it was destroyed by fire on the evening of February 13, 1923. The blaze was thought to have originated in the hotel room of a pullman porter who, after pressing his uniform, failed to unplug the electric iron on his way out. It took several hours to control the fire. There were no casualties that night because Fannie McCarty remained at her switchboard until all occupants had been alerted and evacuated. Only a few offices and the ticket counter were still fit for use. The clock tower stood amidst the blackened stone and brick walls but was toppled two weeks later by severe canyon winds. Falling bricks killed clerk Frank Yentzer.

The third Station, the one that stands today, rose from the ruin. Los Angeles architects John and Donald Parkinson were commissioned to design a new station using the old foundation. At the huge cost of $400,000.00, it opened May 22, 1924 with bands playing and orators praising crews for the rapid reconstruction. The two story structure is 374 feet long and averaged 88 feet wide. It's roof is of red Cordova Mission tile, the walls built of buff-pink brick made in Ogden. Reflecting an Italian Renaissance style, its four Wall Avenue doorways are trimmed with carved Boise sandstone and wrought iron embellishments. A study of the carvings reveals clusters of fruit and over each entrance is a carved buffalo as it appears on the Buffalo nickel. The main lobby, called the Grand Lobby, is 60 by 112 feet and 56 feet from floor to ridgepoles. High cross beams are made from massive Oregon Douglas Fir timbers.

In 1924 the main floor restaurant had 51 counter seats and tables for 100 patrons. There was a large baggage room, barber shop, men's smoking room, women's rest area, and an emergency medical facility. The ticket counter was on the east side; Western Union Telegraph and Station Master offices were at the south end; and the Union Newsstand was situated along the west wall. Big doors opened onto the waiting platform with a subway connecting eight covered tracks.

This basic configuration was retained through the hectic days of World War II when thousands of G. I.'s stopped in Ogden to enjoy the city's hospitality. However, by the time of the 1969 celebration of the Golden Spike Centennial, it had become apparent that the future of this magnificent building was threatened. With the decline of rail travel, the facility had decayed to the point of demolition. There was talk of razing the building and the wrecking ball was waiting in the wings.

Not wanting to see this extraordinary piece of Americana be destroyed, the community took action. Ogden leaders wrote to officials of the Ogden Union Railway and Depot Company asking that the building be given to them. In 1977, after several false starts and mis-understandings, the City of Ogden received title to the building. About this same time the building was nominated and accepted by the National Register of Historic Sites. With these two hurdles out of the way, the community rallied and funding was found through private and public means. Renovation began in earnest and the result is the building we see today, structurally and aesthetically true to its original design.

Today Ogden's Union Station is a cultural, social, and civic gathering place. It's generous and hospitable space houses four museums; the Utah State Railroad Museum and the Eccles Rail Center, the John M. Browning Firearms Museum, the Browning/Kimball Antique Car Museum, the Museum of Natural History, as well as the Gallery at the Station and the M.S. Browning Theater. Also inside the visitor will find the Wattis-Dumke Model railroad, gift shop, U. S. Forest Service Visitors center, the City/County Visitors Bureau, The Union Grill Restaurant and Warren's Train Shop all sitting as the anchor to the notorious historical 25th Street with its's shops, restaurants and nightclubs.

SPENCER S. AND HOPE FOX ECCLES
RAIL CENTER

The Spencer S. and Hope Fox Eccles Rail Center (located on the south end of Ogden's Union Station) showcases some of the equipment that was used to overcome the immense spaces and geographical challenges of the west. Many of these giants appear in this book as envisioned through the eyes of an artist and described by the pen of a historian. You can see the Gas Turbine diesel electric engine, designed to power up the grades of the Wasatch Mountains, the Northern Steam Locomotive #833, used to move people, mail, and commerce through the west, and Big Hook, a crane with the lifting capacity of 250,000 pounds, pulled out whenever the call came in "We have one on the ground!" This equipment is displayed so that the visitor to the Utah State Railroad Museum can see the immensity of the equipment that was needed to conquer the Rockies and the Great Basin of the American West.

If you are traveling the west please come to visit the Spencer S. and Hope Fox Eccles Rail Center at Ogden's Union Station to view the display and let your imagination roam.

Photo by Chris Bojanower

— Glossary —

ALCO:

Stands for American Locomotive Company. This company built many steam and diesel locomotives from 1847-1969.

Challenger:

A steam locomotive with a 4-6-6-4 wheel arrangement.

Coal Burner:

A locomotive that burns coal to heat water into steam.

Consolidation:

A steam locomotive with a 2-8-0 wheel arrangement.

Cylinder:

The large boxy looking area in the front of a steam locomotive that supplies expanded steam to the pistons to drive a locomotive. Defined in cross section and thrust length such as 30 inches x 34 inches.

DDA-40X:

The real term for the "Centennial " diesel electric locomotive. DD standing for two 4-axle trucks , **"A"** means it has a cab to drive the locomotive, **40X** relates to the electrical and engine information.

Drivers:

The large wheels on a locomotives. Regular sizes were as small as 36 inches and as large as 84 inches.

Double-Stack:

A railcar that is designed to carry two containers, such as truck trailers, stacked one on top of the other.

Engineer:

The person who drives a locomotive.

Fireman:

The man that tends to the fire on a steam locomotive.

Flanger:

A larger steel blade that can be lowered to clean snow and ice between rails.

Gradient:

The vertical rise over a 100 foot horizontal run. 1.14 percent = 1.14 feet of vertical rise in 100 feet of horizontal run.

Horsepower:

(HP) A power rate of 550-foot pounds per second (about 1 1/3 times the actual power of a horse.)

Jordan Spreader:

A railroad car built by Jordan that contains pneumatically-powered blades to move snow or earth.

Lash-up:

Two or more locomotives coupled together on the same train.

MAC:

An acronym standing for **M** a wide or safety cab on a locomotive and **AC** standing for **alternating current** to drive the locomotives electric motors.

Medium:

Material used by an artist to paint or draw a picture or painting.

MPH:

Miles per hour

Oil:

Used as a paint when a color pigment is mixed with oil. Paint is mixed and thinned by oil or oil products.

Oil Burner:

A steam locomotive that uses waste oil to heat water into steam.

PA:

*A locomotive built by ALCO for passenger service. **P** denoting **p**assenger locomotive and **A** that it has a cab.*

psi:

***P**ounds per **s**quare **i**nch.*

Pilot:

A person who commands a group to move a vehicle as a team.

SD-40-2:

*A common locomotive that has 3000 hp built by General Motors. **SD** denoting **S**pecial **D**uty and the **-40-2** relates to the electrical and engine information.*

Shay:

A gear-driven steam locomotive that was built to run over light rail and handle tight curves. The drive shaft is located on the engineer's side to power the trucks.

TOFC:

***T**railers **O**n **F**lat **C**ars. Also known as Piggy back or "Van" trains.*

Tractive Effort/Force:

The amount of force a locomotive exerts against the rail at the driving wheel. It is a theoretical figure: boiler pressure times the square of the cylinder diameter times the piston stroke divided by the driver diameter.

Truck:

The unit that holds the axles on a locomotive, railcar or trolley. The unit can be powered as on a locomotive, or non-powered as on a railcar.

Unit:

A term used often to describe a locomotive.

Waste Oil:

The leftovers derived from the making of petroleum products. The substance can burn but only at high temperatures. Known to most as "tar" it was used for road-ways and also for use in steam and turbine locomotives. In the late 1960's advanced chemical engineering changed waste oil to be used in making other petroleum products.

Watercolor:

A mix of color pigments and other chemicals that turns to a water-based paint. The colors are thinned and mixed with water.

Whyte System:

The system used to describe differing classes of steam locomotives by the locomotives wheel count. As an example, a 2-8-2 had two small guide wheels or pony wheels, eight large drive wheels and two more wheels that support the firebox or tailing wheels. The American count uses the wheel while the European count uses the axles. As an example, an American 2-8-2 would be known as a 1-4-1 in Europe. Some of locomotives that had class names follow:

0-4-0, 0-6-0, 0-8-0 = Switchers	2-10-2 = Santa Fe
4-4-0 = American	2-10-4 = Texas
2-6-6-6 = Allegheny	4-10-2 = Southern Pacific
4-6-0 = Ten Wheeler	4-12-2 = Union Pacific
2-8-8-4 = Yellowstone	4-6-6-4 = Challenger
4-6-2 = Pacific	
4-8-8-4 = Big Boy	
4-6-4 = Hudson	
4-8-2 = Mountain	
4-8-4 = Northern	
2-6-0 = Mogul	
2-6-2 = Prairie	
2-8-0 = Consolidation	
2-8-2 = Mikado	
2-8-4 = Berkshire	

— Railroad Museums and Tourist Lines in Utah —

To learn more about the railroad history of Utah, as well as various rail-oriented museums and operating railroad lines that can be visited on site in the state, the following organizations can be contacted for further information:

Ogden Union Station Museum (State Railroad Museum of Utah), 2501 Wall Avenue, Ogden, Utah 84401, (801) 629-8444.

Heber Valley Railroad (operating steam passenger railway), P.O. Box 609, Heber City, Utah 84032, (435) 654-5601.

Golden Spike National Historic Site, Promontory Summit, P.O. Box 897, Brigham City, Utah 84302, (435) 471-2209.

National Railway Historical Society, Promontory Chapter, 1965 W. Lindsay Drive, Taylorsville, Utah 84119, (801) 968-8080.

Railway & Locomotive Historical Society, Golden Spike Chapter, 3670 Quincy Avenue, #106, Ogden, Utah 84403, (801)621-8400.

Utah State Historical Society, 300 Rio Grande Street, Salt Lake City, Utah 84101, (801) 533-3500.

Tooele County Museum, 35 N. Broadway, Tooele, Utah 84074, (435) 882-2836.

Western Mining and Railroad Museum, 296 S. Main, Helper, Utah 84526, (435) 472-3009.

Historic Brigham City Depot Museum
800 W. Forest Street, Brigham City, Utah 84302,
(435) 723-2989

— About the Artist and the Author —

Gilbert H. Bennett grew up in Salt Lake City where his interest in railroads started in his childhood. His grandfather worked for the Chicago & Northwestern Railway as a freight agent in Salt Lake City. As such, Gil's father became enamored with railroads and the fascination with trains was passed down. Gil's father would often take the family down to the yards to watch trains as they arrived and departed. During the many visits to the yards, Gil began to draw the various locomotives he encountered. His talent for drawing accurate and detailed objects emerged quickly.

Many times Gil would pass the time of day drawing his favorite subjects—trains. As time passed, pursuits other than art occupied Gil's time, but the love of drawing persisted. He was introduced to oil painting while attending the University of Utah where he studied Architecture, as well as Western and Far Eastern art. He has been selling his art work since 1984 and graduated with a Bachelor of Fine Arts Degree from the University of Utah in 1988. From that time, his art has appeared on calendars, magazine and book covers as well as "Leanin Tree" and "Wasatch Greeting" Christmas cards. His work is known internationally and is sought after by railroad enthusiasts as well as art collectors. His art reflects the influence of the late Howard Fogg as well as the great masters Renoir, Rubens and Titian. Although his artistic interests are diverse, his specialty—by choice—is railroading. Each painting Gil does is meticulously researched. In the words of one collector,…"Gil counts the nuts and bolts so you don't have to." Whether utilizing his own first hand research, or railroad materials and photographs from his clients' collections, the level of detail is both accurate and artistically rendered. The same thorough research applies to the setting and scenery surrounding the railroad subject, making each painting a piece of art. Gil is a member of The Society of Steam Era Artists of America. His oils and watercolors have appreciated considerably in value with the passage of time. Simply put, whether steam or diesel, whether in oil or watercolor, his work uniquely captures the spirit and grandeur of American railroading. Gilbert currently lives in Lehi, Utah with his wife, Gayleen and two sons. You are welcome to visit his web site at: www.trainz.cc.

Photo by Charles Trentelman

Stephen L. Carr was born, raised and attended schools in Salt Lake City. He then graduated from the University of Utah and went on to obtain an M.D. degree from George Washington University School of Medicine in Washington, D.C. He and his wife, Ruth, live in Holladay, Utah, where he also has a pediatric practice.

He has enjoyed a life-long interest in Utah history, especially railroads and ghost towns. He authored the books, *The Historical Guide to Utah Ghost Towns* and *Utah Ghost Rails*, a book about the abandoned railroads of the state, and was designer and cartographer of the *Map of Utah Railroads*. He also wrote a book concerning the history of Holladay called *Holladay-Cottonwood Places and Faces*.

He has been an instructor on Utah ghost towns with the University of Utah, Division of Continuing Education and Brigham Young University Education Week. He was a member and the historian of the Governor's "Philo T. Farnsworth for Statuary Hall Commission" and wrote and compiled a book on the history of Mr. Farnsworth for the U.S. House of Representatives' Statuary Hall.

Dr. Carr serves as a member of the Board of Directors and is the Historian of the Heber Valley Railroad and has written books for tourists riding on this steam railroad. He is Chairman of the Utah Committee for Geographic Names. He is also the editor of *The Golden Spike*, the newsletter of the Promontory Chapter of the National Railway Historical Society. He is a Life Member of the Utah State Historical Society, the Colorado Railroad Museum and the Feather River Rail Society as well as a member of the Utah State Railroad Museum and Union Pacific Historical Society.

When people learn of Dr. Carr's extensive interest and association with railroads, many have asked him why he went into medicine instead of railroading. After much thought about the question, he has no answer, and in fact has often wondered the same thing himself.

— References —

Alder, Caine, editor, *Utah State Rail Plan,* Transportation Planning Division, Utah Dept. of Transportation, Salt Lake City, Utah.

Best, Gerald M., *Iron Horses to Promontory,* Golden West Books, San Marino, California.

Burns, A.J., and Burns, J.F., compilers, *The Official Guide of the Railways and Steam Navigation Lines of the United State, Canada, Puerto Rico, Mexico and Cuba,* 1942 edition, National Railway Publication Company, New York, New York.

Carr, Stephen L., and Edwards, Robert W., *Utah Ghost Rails,* Western Epics, Salt Lake City, Utah.

Cockle, George R., *Centennials in Action,* Overland Publications, Muncie, Indiana.

Cockle, George, R., *Giants of the West,* Overland Publications, Muncie, Indiana.

Combs, Barry B., *Westward to Promontory,* American West Publishing Company, Palo Alto, California.

Edmonson, Harold, and Goodheart, David, *Zephyrs Thru the Rockies,* Goodheart Publications, Chicago, Illinois.

Ehernberger, James L., and Gschwind, Francis G., *Smoke Over the Divide,* E&G Publications, Callaway, Nebraska.

Gwynn, J. Wallace, editor, *Great Salt Lake,* Utah Geological and Mineral Survey, Bulletin 116, Salt Lake City, Utah.

Heimburger, Donald J., *Rio Grande Steam Locomotives - Standard Gauge,* Heimburger House Publishing Company, River Forest, Illinois.

Kerr, O.M., *Illustrated Treasury of the American Locomotive Company,* W.W. Norton & Company, New York, New York.

Kratville, William W., *Big Boy,* Barnhart Press, Omaha, Nebraska.

Kratville, William W., *The Challenger Locomotives,* Kratville Publications, Omaha, Nebraska.

Kratville, William W., *Golden Rails,* Kratville Publications, Omaha, Nebraska.

Kratville, William W., *The Mighty 800,* Kratville Publications, Omaha, Nebraska.

Kratville, William W., *The Union Pacific Streamliners,* Kratville Publications, Omaha, Nebraska.

Kratville, William W., and Ranks, Harold E., *Motive Power of the Union Pacific,* Barnhart Press, Omaha, Nebraska.

Lathrop, Gilbert A., *Little Engines and Big Men,* The Caxton Printers, Ltd., Caldwell, Idaho.

Lee, Thomas R., *Turbines Westward,* T. Lee Publications, Manhattan, Kansas.

LeMassena, Robert A., *Articulated Steam Locomotives of North America,* Sundance Publications, Denver, Colorado.

LeMassena, Robert A., *Rio Grande to the Pacific,* Sundance Publications, Denver, Colorado.

Metcalfe, Terry, *Union Pacific Modeler,* Metcalfe Publications, Englewood, Colorado.

Myrick, David F., *Railroads of Nevada and Eastern California,* Howell-North Books, Berkeley, California.

Rattenne, Ken, *The Feather River Route Two, A Geographical Tour: Keddie to Salt Lake City,* Trans-Anglo Books, Glendive, California.

Richardson, Robert W., and Hauck, Cornelius W., *Locomotives of the Rio Grande,* Colorado Railroad Museum, Golden, Colorado.

Signor, John R., *The Los Angeles & Salt Lake Railroad Company,* Golden West Books, San Marino, California.

Stagner, Lloyd E., *Union Pacific Motive Power in Transition,* South Platte Press, David City, Nebraska.

Stewart, John J, *The Iron Trail to the Golden Spike,* Deseret Book Company, Salt Lake City, Utah.

Strack, Don, *Ogden Rails,* Golden Spike Chapter, Railway & Locomotive Historical Society, Ogden, Utah.

Swett, Ira L., *Interurbans of Utah,* Interurban Press, Cerritos, California.

Tippie, Lester L., President, Promontory Chapter - National Railway Historical Society, Salt Lake City, Utah.

Watson, James W., and Wagner, F. Hol, Jr., *Emil Albrecht's Union Pacific Small Steam Power,* Great American Railroad Photographer Series, Motive Power Services, Nebraska.